AF557818

PMO

PMO

Prime Minister's Office

Through the Years

Himanshu Roy

RUPA

Published by
Rupa Publications India Pvt. Ltd 2025
7/16, Ansari Road, Daryaganj
New Delhi 110002

Sales centres:
Bengaluru Chennai
Hyderabad Jaipur Kathmandu
Kolkata Mumbai Prayagraj

P-ISBN: 978-93-6156-920-3
E-ISBN: 978-93-6156-738-4

First impression 2025

10 9 8 7 6 5 4 3 2 1

Printed in India

In memory of Shakti Sinha
Former Director, Prime Ministers' Museum and Library

Contents

Preface ix

Introduction xix

Congress Years 1

The Non-Congress Years 41

Comparison: England, Canada and Australia 75

Conclusion 99

Annexure I 111

Annexure II 113

Annexure III 117

Endnotes 131

Bibliography 139

Index 143

Preface

For decades, there has been curiosity among the reading public to know about the Prime Minister's Office (PMO): how it functions, the kind of people there, and what their powers are. Is it a typical government office with routine functioning or is there something unique about it? And most importantly, how much power does it have?

For the past 75 years, since 15 August 1947, the Prime Minister's Secretariat (PMS)—renamed the Prime Minister's Office (PMO) in 1977—has been in existence in India. Its historical trajectory with a distant comparison can be located in the appointment of the four private secretaries (PS) of Warren Hastings, the first Governor-General of Colonial India, in 1774.[1] Since then, the private office of the governor-general has been in existence and expanding. The Governor-General's Executive Council (EC), which was also formed in 1774 with four members, has had a separate trajectory. Later, the members were assigned different portfolios (precursor to ministries) with different administrative departments. Both the trajectories, of PSs and the EC, have existed parallel to each other with elementary linkages. The PS of governor-generals, later viceroys, coordinated the works of the EC. However, it was only during Lord Wavell's time that the Cabinet Secretariat (CS) *per se* was formed. In the interim government (2 September 1946–14 August 1947), the PMS was non-existent. Both the secretariats, the PMS and the CS, in their existing forms and roles, evolved in independent India.

However, books with a history of these institutions are rare; at best, there are chapters and articles in some books and journals or a few doctoral theses. Most of the works are memoirs which were written for a particular period. Any work tracking the PMO's organizational lineage, genesis and formation and the reasons behind its importance is lacking. The growing importance of the organisation, since 1964, which has a built-in memory of departmental-ministerial records, has created curiosity among the reading public to know more about it: Jarnail Singh's memoir *With Four Prime Ministers* (2020), Wajahat Habibullah's *My Years With Rajiv* (2020), N.K. Singh's memoir *Portrait of Power* (2020), and Pranab Mukherjee's *My Presidential Years* (2021) are the latest additions[2] to the genre that partially bridge the gap.

It is assumed that the importance of the PMO is inevitable in the prime ministerial form of government, which, in turn, is inevitable in the cabinet form of parliamentary democracy. It is also argued that in the nuclearized and globalized world, realizing this inevitability is imperative for the efficient and effective functioning of the government. Additionally, it is related to the growing democratization of society, which is clamouring for more decentralized polity and delegation of powers.

The PMO eclipsing the cabinet and the CS has definitely been under public scrutiny during the tenures of the three prime ministers of the Nehru's family, who played defining roles in the development of the prime ministerial government, leading to the realized importance of the PMO. However, while in other times, particularly in the decades of the coalition governments, the cabinet and the CS acquired greater prominence, a dent to their importance remained. The approach to interpreting the development, and importance, of the PMO as inevitable is therefore contentious, if not fallacious, as it has transcended the cabinet and its secretariat in terms of relevance.

In the British tradition, the cabinet and its secretariat remain sacrosanct, despite the increasing prominence of the prime minister. In 1979 and 1997, PM Margaret Thatcher and Tony Blair, respectively, attempted to change the role of the PMS by appointing advisors and empowering them with the mandate to advise and formulate policies, which was the domain of the CS. It was strongly resisted. The advisory roles were subsequently taken off from the PMS during the tenure of PM Gordon Brown. The British academia and reading public still debate over whether the prime ministerial government has come of age or whether it is the cabinet that runs the government. But one thing is certain: the PMS has a lesser role in running the government; its different policy units have been dismantled or reduced in size. Even their roles have been marginalized, with a clear demarcation of their domains. Contrary to this, the development of the PMS in India has seen a phenomenal growth in the post-colonial years.

In India, the prime ministers also kept on changing the designations and ranks of the chief executive officers in the PMS. The rank of the joint secretary in the initial years became the Principal Private Secretary (PPS) during the Nehru regime. The designation was inherited from the British PMS. The PPS to the British PM, however, was equivalent to the rank of the deputy secretary in India, whereas in Britain, the rank was known as the assistant secretary. The post would be occupied by the serving ICS/IAS/IFS officers. Shastri changed the designation from PPS to secretary, while PM Indira Gandhi created a new designation for P.N. Haksar when he retired. He was then designated as the principal secretary, which is a rank that still continues, while retaining the designation of secretary to the PM for P.C. Dhar. The secretary to the PMO still continues; however, Rajiv Gandhi further experimented with the post. Once P.C. Alexander, the principal secretary to Indira Gandhi and Rajiv Gandhi, left, three parliamentary secretaries were appointed instead of a new principal secretary, who eventually was appointed after the former were unable to deliver what was expected of them. The idea was to let them perform the political tasks of the principal secretary in the PMO. The principal secretaries, Haksar and then Alexander, handled both administrative and political responsibilities for Indira Gandhi and Rajiv Gandhi. The scale of their administrative works was leviathan in themselves. Rajiv wanted to segregate the administrative and political functions of the PMS-PMO. In fact, the principal secretary had become the one-man contact point for the PM, and the PMO had become the single-window clearance house of the cabinet. The PMO, thus, had emerged as the powerhouse of the government, unlike in Britain where it was the cabinet secretariat.

During Rajiv Gandhi's tenure, the PMO became bigger in size (in terms of staff numbers) compared to his mother's time. He had also inherited another new precedent initiated by his mother: the appointment of retired civil servants as principal secretaries. When Morarji Desai initiated it by appointing Vidya Shankar as his principal secretary, there was serious opposition to it, but it subsequently became the acceptable operative principle.

Manmohan Singh added a new dimension to the functioning of the PMO, which was not unprecedented. Indira Gandhi had already enacted it during 1973–76, when the Prime Minister House (PMH) emerged as the new power centre. In the following years, a few senior officials of the PMO used to report to Sonia Gandhi, the chairperson of the National Advisory Council (NAC), which became a parallel political power centre, and the actual one; the then PM, the 'rootless wonder', functioned like the principal secretary. The PMO would look after the administrative application of the social policies largely formulated by the NAC. During Rajiv Gandhi's tenure, the application of political decisions was looked after by the three parliamentary secretaries, but it was within the PMO. In the new format, it was his widow, Sonia Gandhi, who was heading a parallel policymaking body, the NAC, separate from the PMO. The PMO ensured the application of the Common Minimum Programme (CMP) and reported back to the NAC.

The PMO, during the non-Congress governments preceding the Vajpayee government, was largely low-key. It was restrained in its relations with different ministries. The cabinet and its secretariat had substantive autonomy. Every ministry file was not routed through the PMO, which was downsized, thereby stopping much of its interference in the ministries and the secretariat. The government was represented by the cabinet, and the administration was coordinated by the cabinet secretariat. The prime ministerial form was restrained by coalition politics and the absence of the Nehru family.

The Vajpayee government was the only non-Congress government which had an active PMO despite being a coalition government. It created a new sub-structure within the PMO. A new post of the National Security Advisor (NSA) and a new National Security Council (NSC) were created that coordinated specifically with the ministries of defence, external affairs and atomic energy. The post of the principal secretary and the NSA was occupied by Brijesh Mishra, who was a 'risk-taker' and strengthened the authority of the PM. It was a classic case of when the cabinet functioned as it did but the PM enjoyed an equally authoritative position.

The Modi government, which succeeded the Manmohan Singh government, has another unique feature. It has the strength of a single-party majority government but runs a coalition government. Unlike earlier, the principal secretary and the NSA are two different positions, occupied by officers holding cabinet ranks. The third officer is the principal advisor. In Modi's first term, the principal secretary was appointed through an ordinance, which was brought in to remove the legal hurdle in his appointment. The PMO has been streamlined with a clear demarcation of roles of the top three officers. The policy inputs and political work are conducted by the NITI Aayog and the party, respectively. It is unlike Indira Gandhi's PMS, wherein Haksar did everything till 1973. But officially, he remained at par with the cabinet secretary as per the warrant of precedence. Now, the principal secretary and the NSA with cabinet ranks are higher than the cabinet secretary. The PM directly interacts with the secretaries, individually and collectively, of different ministries, a precedence initiated by Indira Gandhi. All the important files of the ministries are routed through the PMO, but all the procedures of the cabinet are scrupulously applied.[3] The three principal officers—the principal advisor, the NSA and the principal secretary—report directly to the PM within their demarcated roles.

The appointments of the personal staff (OSD/private secretaries) of ministers were brought under the purview of the Cabinet Committee of Appointments, and their service rules and tenure were streamlined. The staff of the PMO, however, has been exempted.

It is equally pertinent to understand the reasons for this change, from the cabinet form of government to the prime ministerial form of government. While in the Constituent Assembly the debate was surrounding the cabinet form of government, in praxis, Nehru was trying to develop the prime ministerial form, which was being opposed by Patel and others. This dichotomy widened after Patel's death; after the first Lok Sabha election, Nehru gradually began to move towards the prime ministerial form. Shastri learnt it from Nehru and provided an institutional shape by changing the role and status of the PMS, while Indira Gandhi extended its domain to political work. Afterwards, its composition and role remained within this framework. Essentially, when there have been Congress and BJP prime ministers, the governments have been prime ministerial, and the role of the PMO was expanded. When the governments have been of other parties, the roles of the cabinet and its secretariat were expanded.

In Britain, the form of government remains dominated by the cabinet, and its secretariat is the only office which handles the administrative work. The political work is looked after by the parties. The PMS has no role except for providing secretarial assistance to the PM. Despite all the nuclearization and globalization, it remains predominantly in the cabinet form. Many of the prime ministers, despite being charismatic, either lost parliamentary elections or were replaced by the candidates of other parties. Many times, powerful cabinet ministers have rebelled against their prime ministers, and the prime ministers have had to resign.

In India, such situations have been rare, at least within the Congress. In the non-Congress parties, the BJP has better democratic traditions and its prime ministerial candidates have stayed changing, chosen by the party as the consensus candidates. The non-Congress and non-BJP prime ministers were mostly chosen after the elections by the leaders of coalition of parties.

They were mostly not chosen by the electorate. In the case of the BJP or the Congress, it was the electorate who stamped their support or rejected them. That facilitated the development of the prime ministerial government. In Britain, despite the approval of the electorate for the candidatures of the prime ministers, a prime ministerial government did not develop. This has been a stark difference between England and India, and a lesson to be learnt for the democratization of governance and the institutionalization of democracy. Despite plebiscitary politics and personality cults in many of the elections, there has been no substantive change in the role of the PMS in the past 75 years in Britain, as it has occurred in India.

Thus, in the past 55 years, when Shastri enacted a minor administrative change in 1964, the PMS-PMO and the secretary to the PM, called by different names from time to time, became the most important administrative body. It also reflects the marginalization of the cabinet government and its secretariat, and the arrival of the prime ministerial government and its office (PMO).The powers of the CS remain the same, but the informal administrative protocol has changed, giving importance to the PMO which has impacted the collective decision-making process of the cabinet and its policy formulation.

People have immense faith in the PMO, in the sense that they consider this office to be able to solve their routine problems. If one argues that the PMO is just to provide secretarial assistance to the PM to keep him aware of the latest developments in the country and the world, in terms of every aspect of society, no one will probably believe it. And rightly so, as citizens have 'seen' and read in the media about the role of the PMO being responsible for saving the lives of the citizens and providing them with assistance. Therefore, thousands of messages are received by the office every day from citizens seeking help or suggesting ways to the PMO to improve their lives. They treat it as their government and expect from it solutions to their problems, both personal and social.

Earlier, these 'works' were done by the ministries on their own. With their roles being curtailed, the PMO, along with the higher courts, has become the hope of the citizens. It did not happen in a day but over a period of time. What we hear today about the PMO and the general perception about it have evolved over the last 50 years or more. If one PM is to be named for any substantive alteration, it is Indira Gandhi, who changed the nature of the PMO and the government, collectively represented by the cabinet and served by the CS.

If one reads the memoirs of the civil servants who once worked in the PMO or the CS, one can gather that it is the PMO, not the CS, which is the hub of the government. Constitutionally, it's the cabinet, of which the PM is a part, which is the government; in effect, the collective has been replaced by the individual or the family that was visible in its worst form during the Indira Gandhi–Rajiv Gandhi–Manmohan Singh regimes. But what actually transpires in the PMO largely remains confined to a small segmentary domain, while for the procedural, constitutional and legal domains, the cabinet and the ministries are brought into the picture.

Those who have written about the PMS-PMO focused purely on their tenures. Most of them were unaware of the details of the past, including the changing ranks and designations of the PPS, such as secretary, principal secretary, etc., and the historical trajectory of the PMS-PMO.

In the writing of this book, Shakti Sinha, the former director of the Nehru Memorial Museum and Library (NMML), Teen Murti House, and the private secretary (PS) to PM Atal Bihari Vajpayee, was of considerable help in explaining the administrative nuances of the functioning of the PMO. My interactions with Jarnail Singh, the joint secretary (JS) in the PMO, N.N. Vohra, the principal secretary to PM Inder Kumar Gujral, and Sanjay Baru, the media advisor to PM Manmohan Singh, further enriched my work. I thank M.S. Rasgotra, the foreign secretary during Indira Gandhi's time in the 1980s, who helped me understand the application of the foreign policy of the government. I also thank the librarian at NMML, Ajit Kumar, and staff members Annu, Rita and Monika for their active and prompt support, and the librarian at DDUC, Delhi University (DU), Abhijeet Sinha, and staff members Shrikant, Hariom and Amit. Finally, I thank Vikas Kumar, a doctoral scholar in the Department of Political Science, DU, and Anshu Kumar, a doctoral scholar, Centre for Political Studies, Jawaharlal Nehru University (JNU), for their technical assistance. Finally, I thank Rudra Narayan Sharma and Arjit Sharma from Rupa Publications for their constant editorial support and assistance.

Introduction

On 2 September 1946, when the interim government headed by Jawaharlal Nehru was formed, he was officially designated as the vice president (VP) of the Viceroy's Executive Council (EC). The viceroy was himself the president while presiding over the official meeting of the council. The members of the EC were the members Home, Agriculture, Finance, Commerce, Defence, Labour, Industries, Railway, and Mines; the EC functioned under the provision of the 1935 Act.

Nehru tried to function like the prime minister (PM) of the cabinet. But the colonial administration did not let the provisional government function in such a mode; neither was there any Prime Minister's Secretariat (PMS). Viceroy Wavell and Mountbatten did, however, provide the VP and the members of the EC secretarial assistance, as required. For that was the British convention of the cabinet functioning, headed by the PM with no portfolio of their own.

In fact, there was no secretariat of the British cabinet till World War I, and neither did the PM or his secretariat exist even after World War II. The PM didn't keep any portfolio either. Nehru, on the other hand, kept with himself the portfolio of external affairs and looked for a formal secretariat.

The viceroy's EC had no secretariat either. Viceroy Linlithgow had thought of establishing the governor-general's secretariat in 1936, and his private secretary was given the additional designation of secretary to the executive council of the governor-general. But the formation of the secretariat did not materialize. Interestingly, before Viceroy Willingdon, the private secretary to the governor-general, who headed the EC, was not allowed to attend the meetings of the council. It was Willingdon who initiated the practice of letting the secretary attend the council meetings.

In the absence of the executive council secretariat, it was the private secretary of the governor-general/viceroy who coordinated the council meetings (preparing agendas and arranging meetings). In 1774, four members (councillors) were appointed to the council; their meetings were informal, private and secret, and the members wrote their own minutes. There was no secretary. The executive council secretary was appointed only during 1935–36. Till then, the secretaries of each department looked after the papers of their departments—the department was constituted of officers and the subordinate establishment. The officers included the secretary, deputy secretary, under secretary and assistant secretary. Additional secretaries and joint secretaries were appointed to provide relief to secretaries from their heavy workload. Both these officers were next to secretaries in rank. The subordinate establishment included superintendents, assistants, and second- and third-division clerks. At the time of Warren Hastings (1774), there were only five departments: public, secret, revenue, military and inspection. The council met once a week, and the tenure of its members was five years. As the colonial rule expanded to new territories and stabilized, the role of the council and its members expanded. In 1859, the portfolio system was introduced, which was recognized by the 1861 Act. Each member of the council was made in charge of one or more departments.[1] In the subsequent years, it acquired the role and shape of the cabinet, and its secretariat (since 1945) became the cabinet secretariat. After 15 August 1947, it became the dominant office, and the cabinet secretary became the senior-most officer in the administrative hierarchy, replacing the private secretary/chief of staff of the governor-general/viceroy in terms of hierarchy, power and importance. After 1971, the Principal Private Secretary (PPS) to the PM, who was earlier like the private secretary/chief of staff of the governor-general/viceroy, once again began to overshadow the cabinet secretary.

It was during Wavell's tenure, in October 1945, that a small secretariat was created in the EC to primarily service the Coordination Committee of war resources and reconstruction. It was expected to 'develop later into a real secretariat' of the EC, which was till then functioning under Evic Coates, Advisor-Military Finance, and it subsequently developed into 'a proper Cabinet Secretariat', of which Coates was the first cabinet secretary, or the secretary of the EC, and H.M. Patel served as the joint secretary, 'to coordinate the military and civil sides of the Government of India';[2] Patel was to become the first PPS to Nehru within a few months, when the interim government would be formed, and subsequently serve as the cabinet secretary of the EC.

Nehru's Vision for Himself

After the transfer of power on 15 August 1947, Nehru intended to create 'a high-powered (PM) secretariat swamping over the Cabinet Secretariat'. But this was opposed by Sardar Patel and other cabinet colleagues. Even senior officers like H.M. Patel and V.P. Menon opposed it, and Mountbatten too was not in favour. On 14 August, an informal meeting of officers was fixed with Nehru, on the advice of Sardar Patel, to deliberate upon his idea of the PMS, in which Lord Ismay's advice, which was sought by

H.M. Patel, was placed before him for his perusal.[3] Nehru read the letter and listened to the ideas of the officers. That probably persuaded him to drop the idea of creating a formal organization of the PMS following the pattern of the cabinet secretariat, but with more powers.

Nehru was probably visualizing himself in place of the viceroy, and his private secretariat was to be replaced by the PMS, while the Executive Council Secretariat (the cabinet secretariat) was to play the advisory role. It was reflective of his thinking of a way to transcend the cabinet to make the PM more powerful. Initially, Nehru used to include his PPS in the cabinet meetings, which was not the norm as per the British PMS. The practice was stopped when it was disliked by his cabinet colleagues and the officers of the cabinet secretariat.

He was following the tradition of the viceroy, whose private secretary used to attend the EC meetings. Earlier, during the interim government, he emphasized the cabinet mode of functioning. One may recall his letter[4] to Viceroy Wavell, or Lord Wavell's letter[5] to his British monarch, where he even suggested that Rajaji, his colleague in the government, functioned like a cabinet minister by not reporting any cabinet matter directly to the viceroy. However, once the transfer of power took place, his focus shifted from the cabinet government to a prime ministerial government. The intention, thus, was not to function in the cabinet style or the collective mode; on the contrary, it was to put himself in the position of the viceroy, or, at best, as an elected viceroy like an American president, with his cabinet colleagues as his aides, akin to the EC, who were to report to him. His functioning, including his presidential years in the Congress, if analyzed closely, reflects a particular trait in his personality that was not reflective of collective functioning and responsibility. It revealed a more individualistic trait that did not allow him to accept his contemporaries as his leaders or even team members; neither was he willing to work as a subordinate or accept criticism. Even when he was not elected as the president of the Congress in 1946, he did not back out, for the president of the Congress was to become the PM. He never offered to accept the elected president, Patel, as his leader who was to become the ex-officio prime minister of India; finally, Gandhi had to intervene and ask Patel to step back. Nehru's intolerance was reflected early in 1951, when he initiated the first constitutional amendment to muzzle the voices of criticism that the Congress government was facing for extra-judicial killings and other acts. The local government in Madras had banned *Cross Road*, a weekly journal, which won the case in court against the ban. To overrule this judgement, the law was amended.

Emergence of the Prime Ministerial Government

In the fourteen years following Patel's death, the collective functioning of the cabinet gradually declined. In its place, the prime ministerial government emerged, and with it emerged the PMS. The PMS, however, was still providing only secretarial assistance; governmental activities, policy formulation and supervision were still being coordinated by the cabinet secretariat. This was unlike the period post 1964, when the role of the PMS was changed by PM Lal Bahadur Shastri, as they began to advise and coordinate political, ministerial and administrative work with an institutionalized repository of data from the ministries. It transcended all the boundaries of federal and cabinet functioning, and subsequently also began to overlook, supervise and coordinate the developmental works of the states in an institutionalized way. It was thus the gradual expansion of the role of the PMS after Nehru, which was much more than the assigned works of secretarial assistance visualized during the interim government. It was not an ad-hoc, episodic, one-time phenomenon or event that the PMS had embarked on after the change of its role by Shastri.

Now the point is how do we look at its role; whether the PMS should provide only secretarial assistance to the PM, as it was during Nehru's time, or whether it should operate in an all-pervasive institutionalized way, as it has developed in India since 1964? Two distinct and contrary interpretations can be found among writers who have worked on the PMS: one section supports the post-1964 emergence of the PMS as an essential part of the contemporary Westminster model, which has become prime ministerial in form; the other section emphasizes the minimization of its role. But both agree that the role of the PMS is more than providing secretarial assistance to the PM amid the changing complexities of government functioning in India and the world. During Nehru's tenure, civil servants felt that there was a lack of coordination between the PM and the cabinet secretariat. There were opposing responses in terms of what Nehru used to say verbally when asked for approval by the civil servants, and what he did when the papers were put before him. It led to a lot of extra paperwork and waste of time that delayed the formal approval of work. To avoid it, the PMS was strengthened during Shastri's tenure. Shastri had observed it closely when he had looked after the cabinet secretariat in 1964 as a minister without a portfolio.

The emergence of the prime ministerial form of government and the marginalization of the cabinet was not questioned, which became the root cause for the emergence of an all-pervasive PMS; it was Nehru who was primarily responsible for it, as he visualized himself, as stated earlier, as an American president or an elected viceroy, and his cabinet members as his aides to be removed at will if they did not function to his liking. He never visualized himself as a British PM, just heading the cabinet as a coordinator, where the cabinet and parliament were more important than the PM. He also did not see the two functioning as collective institutions as representatives of the citizens. The citizens aren't just the electorate providing legitimacy to the government; rather, they are the government.

To Nehru, the parliament and the cabinet were debating platforms providing ideas for better governance. The government, no doubt, was the collective will of the citizens; but its form was to be prime ministerial, and not up to the cabinet, which was the manifestation of his individualistic trait visible from his Congress presidential years. It was this trait which led to the emergence of the dynasty, also present in his father Motilal Nehru who had requested Gandhi in 1928 to make his son Jawaharlal the next Congress president after him.[6] After Patel died in 1950, this trait became more pronounced and visible, best reflected in Nehru making his daughter Indira Gandhi the president of the Congress in 1959.

In 1946, when the interim government was formed in India, and subsequently, when power was transferred in 1947, Britain had a cabinet government and cabinet secretariat, with all the powers vested in it. 'The Prime Minister's Secretariat, (on the other hand), was designated as personal office not classified as a department.'[7] It reflected the conventional positions of the PM and the cabinet in England. The PM did not head a ministry;

in running the affairs of the government, he was advised by the cabinet secretary and not the PMS, which had no jurisdiction over it; therefore, the PMS had a very small number of staff headed by the PPS, who held a rank equivalent to the senior deputy secretary.

Since the PM was advised by the ministers, the resignation of a few senior ministers made the government unstable, posing a challenge to the leadership of the PM in the party. The cabinet, therefore, also reflected the political equation of its members in the party; in other words, senior party leaders were the senior members of the cabinet, who were consulted by the PM in the formation of ministries, policymaking, and running the government.

Hence, this shows that the government in England was a collective, which it continues to be still. Moreover, despite elements of the prime ministerial form sneaking into the system over the decades, it is the control of the party that impacts government formation, substantively retaining a cabinet government.

PMS and the Cabinet

When Nehru visualized the PMS swamping the cabinet secretariat, he was indicating the impending prime ministerial government engulfing the cabinet. In fact, he remarked in the cabinet, in 1950, that 'Cabinet or no cabinet, so long as I am Prime Minister I will carry out the policy.'[8] Patel and other cabinet colleagues opposed him on the principle that it was the cabinet, not the PM, which was all-powerful. The PM is just first among equals, the coordinator of the cabinet; he may initiate policy formulation but the ultimate custodian and repository of all acts is the cabinet, the collective, and not the PM, the individual. The PM was not the boss or the final word; neither was the PMS 'the miniature government within the government of India'.[9]

Babasaheb Ambedkar was even critical of the working style of the cabinet, which he felt had 'become a merely recording and registration office of decisions already arrived at by (its) Committees',[10] which was a contrarian view to that of Attlee, who felt that the committee provides in-depth views on subjects of which ministers may be unaware. So, for better policymaking, Attlee felt that it was necessary. This was a new development then and subsequently became a standard operating feature of the cabinet functioning as the cabinet secretariat, a post that had become an integral part of the cabinet after 1916. The PMS, however, was yet to swamp over the cabinet secretariat in England; in fact, to date, it is the cabinet secretariat which has the dominant role. The PMO, legally speaking, is not a department; it provides only secretarial assistance to the PM. Yet it's the most important office, as over the decades the nature of the government has become practically prime ministerial. From the first among equals, it has become a modified version of the role of an American president. It is no longer the cabinet that determines the direction and the running of the government. Its role has shrunk to primarily catering to the institutional and procedural formalities in a single-party government.

The pertinent point here is to analyze the reasons for this change in the relationship between the PM and the cabinet. For that one has to analyze the personality-oriented plebiscitary mode of election campaigns and their linkages with the Indian electorate dominantly constituting of the peasantry. Nehru began the personality-oriented process in 1952, and Indira Gandhi introduced the plebiscitary mode in 1971 while retaining her father's approach. Eventually, a combination of both persisted and it continues to date.

But it has not been a unilinear process. There have been periods when not the personality but issues have dominated election campaigns, and the electorate has voted for the issues while overlooking the personality-oriented contest. Many times, personalities and issues have combined to result in certain parties winning and their prime ministerial candidates getting overwhelming seats in the Lok Sabha.

Its consequence has not been good for the democratization of the institutions. Nehru began the process for prime ministerial governments and wanted a grand PMS. Shastri created the grand PMS, and using it as a tool, he tried to create the prime ministerial government through the backdoor. Indira Gandhi initially used the PMS for herself and subsequently used her image for electoral victory. Once she succeeded in the 1971 general elections, she combined the two—the PMS and the electoral victory—to transform the nature of her government into the prime ministerial form. She further attached the assistants of the PMS with Sanjay Gandhi and began to ask her cabinet ministers and officers to meet him. This precedence was followed by the Manmohan Singh government when Pulok Chatterjee, the joint secretary in the PMO, was reporting to Sonia Gandhi, the chairperson of the National Advisory Council (NAC).

In England, charismatic personalities like Churchill or Margaret Thatcher could not succeed in creating a sustained prime ministerial government except during their tenures. Either they lost the election or were replaced by others in their parties despite having been the prime ministers. Sometimes there was a rebellion by their cabinet colleagues who had a grip over the parties, or there was turmoil within the parties against their prime ministers. Both kinds of rebellion reflect the point that the PM is not the boss, just the first among equals. The average prime ministerial tenure is approximately ten years. Either they are voted out by the electorate or the party or the cabinet.

The institutionalization of democracy has evolved over the centuries in England, but it is yet to strengthen itself in India. Here the parties or the cabinet are more pliable to the leadership if the leadership brings them to power. The opposite of it—the prolonged absence of a party from power—may breed rebellion within a party or against the leadership. In England, party leaders who are also part of the cabinet command popular support and are in a position to assume the mandate of leadership.

In India, this backbone of popular support for leaders in the cabinet was broken by design by Nehru under the Kamaraj Plan, and later by Indira Gandhi through different mechanisms within the party and the government, helped by the PMS. It led to the cabinet members' dependence on Nehru or Indira Gandhi for their ministerial berths. The more the ministers became rootless, the more pliable they became, leading to the strengthening of the prime ministerial government. The collective functioning of the cabinet gradually became redundant. The process was started by Nehru to foist his daughter into the position of leadership; thus, the Congress presidency and the Kamaraj Plan were a part of it.

In the absence of any universal, pan-Indian radical social movements in the post-colonial years, the political leaders emerging out of electoral politics were more concerned about their political careers, constituencies and castes. The movements that emerged were sectional and regional, lacking universal characteristics;

except for the Congress, no other political party had pan-Indian acceptance. The BJP has emerged in such a mould only in the past ten years. The Janata Party, an amalgamation of four parties, was the result of the Emergency. Its leaders were either already known or gained a significant stature in the aftermath of the Emergency for having been jailed for protesting. So when its government was formed, it was not prime ministerial; similar was the case with V.P. Singh's government.

Succinctly, it can be said that governments emerging out of the wombs of universal social movements, not out of regular electoral politics, are more democratic and collective than the prime ministerial type. On the other hand, when representatives dependent on political dynasties are voted into power and treated as messiahs by the electorate to deliver them from their tribulations, the result is the fostering of prime ministerial/chief ministerial governments. Such dynastic governments keep the masses stuck in the status quo but keep raising their illusionary hopes for the next election.

These political dynasties are more dangerous for democracies, as they foster parliamentary cretinism among the political leaders to keep them dependent on themselves for governmental power. While the cabinet means the will of the collective, the plural, the representatives of the diverse, the prime ministerial form represents the magistracy of one, or at best, the benevolence of one till the next election, which is contrary to the the idea of collective governance in a democracy. This magistracy and benevolence of one is reflected in the form and functioning of the PMO, which is the mirror image of the stature of the PM.

Nehru and Patel

After Patel's death, Nehru became the final word, and his style of functioning made the government prime ministerial in nature. The PMS, however, remained for personal secretarial assistance, set in the British mould. It was yet to emerge as a miniature government.

In this context, it's worth citing the letters written by Nehru and Patel to Gandhi in 1948 regarding the role of the PM. Nehru wrote that 'the PM should have full freedom to act when and how he chooses' in the context of the supervision and coordination of the functioning of the ministries; otherwise 'there will be no cohesion in the Cabinet and the Government'.[11] Patel did not agree with Nehru's statement. In his opinion, it was 'wholly opposed to democratic and cabinet system of government.' He didn't envisage any overriding powers of the PM over his colleagues; 'if he had any, a Cabinet and Cabinet responsibility would be superfluous… This is also…in accord with the UK practice.'[12] Patel had argued that if Nehru's position on the role of the PM was accepted, it would make the PM a 'virtual dictator'. Nehru, on the contrary, felt that his position on the powers of the PM was also in consonance with the practice in the UK.[13]

To clarify, the British cabinet, however, ensured that 'the leading figures of the ruling party and government reach decisions on matters of complex inter-departmental concerns'.[14] Some of its characteristics were 'coordinating ministers', creating 'coherent and structured committee systems', appointing an 'effective Cabinet secretariat', and '[having] a Prime Minister working through the cabinet system'.[15] Attlee believed that the prime minister's basic function was 'to ensure that the Cabinet makes decisions', which would be actuated by different committees chaired by senior cabinet ministers, thereby also lessening the personal involvement of the PM.[16] Many of his recommendations,[17] however, were not applied.

The emergence of the prime ministerial government and the PMS was not a structural or systemic requirement, nor was it the requirement of the time, as civil servants claim in their memoirs.[18] It was an administrative tool for political dominance—the outcome of the desire of the PM, the individual. Nehru did not build up the PMS after opposition from his colleagues and civil servants, but he in turn marginalized the cabinet. Shastri built up the PMS; it was his tool for political dominance and the result of an instrumentalist approach as he lacked the political stature of Nehru. In the absence of Nehru's aura and authority, he used the PMS to make for a prime ministerial form of government. Had the approach been to strengthen the cabinet government, the gap between the PM and the cabinet that existed during Nehru's time would have been bridged. Or had it been a systemic necessity, Britain would have adopted it earlier, akin to the Americans who had to add innovations to the presidency because of the problems faced by the confederation of states for a decade after their War of Independence.

The systemic development of checks and balances in England disallowed the centralization of power into the hands of the PM. In India, after Patel's passing, the system of checks and balances did not evolve either in the cabinet or in the party. Even the resistance of civil servants petered out in the absence of political backing. The fragmentation of the political opposition facilitated the concentration of this power. Subsequently, the PMS became the permanent feature that reinforced the prime ministerial form, feeding on the support of each other to keep the cabinet and its secretariat in the margins.

PMS after Nehru

After the death of Nehru in 1964, Shastri changed the character of the PMS while retaining its name. Nehru had changed the position of the PM after the death of Patel in 1950, but he retained the essential functioning of the PMS, which was to provide secretarial assistance to the PM. It remained the 'gatherers and conveyers…' In short, the staff remained just 'mechanics men'.[19] It remained a 'personal secretariat' till 1960, and was 'not classified as a department'. The staff was 'not responsible for advising on policy or for executing the Prime Minister's decisions on policy.'[20] The rank of his PPS was joint secretary. The rank of the PPS of Attlee, a British PM, was assistant secretary, equivalent to the senior deputy secretary in India.

Shastri changed the form and the mandate of the functioning of the PMS. His PPS was rechristened as secretary to the PM, with a position, according to the Warrant of Precedence, equivalent to that of the cabinet secretary in the government of India. The PMS, visible in the Allocation of Business Rules, 1961, was to facilitate 'the work of consultation and coordination with other ministries…apart from (assisting) the prime minister on important matter[s].'[21] Michael Brecher claimed that L.K. Jha, the secretary to the PM, had told him in an interview that 'the main function of the Secretariat…is to prepare drafts of important speeches, statements and letters.'[22] B.N. Tandon, the joint secretary in the PMS of Indira Gandhi in the early 1970s, later stated that the PMS was 'to assist the Prime Minister in every possible way…

initiating new policies, review[ing] of the working of different ministries, keeping an eye on the Centre-State relations, [and] providing different viewpoints on the proposals received from different ministers for the Cabinet.'

'The Secretariat consists of two parts: one, the regular secretariat where the senior officials work, and the other the prime minister's residence where some secretarial assistance is available. The officials of the PM's secretariat go to the prime minister's house (PMH) as needed.'[23]

The emergence of a parallel 'secretariat' at the PMH from 1974 onwards was a new development. It was the PMH that began to decide and impact the policies of the government. The decision to impose the Emergency was not known even to the PMS. Indira Gandhi had attached two assistants from the PMS to Sanjay Gandhi, who used to make decisions on behalf of the cabinet; more importantly, she used to encourage her cabinet colleagues to meet Sanjay for providing guidance. It was like chickens coming home to roost. As the PMS had swamped the cabinet secretariat earlier, now the PMH swamped the PMS.

In Name Only

When Morarji Desai became the PM in 1977, he partially rolled back the 'powers' of the PMS, which had acquired the status of a 'super cabinet', 'mini government', etc. He began by changing its nomenclature to Prime Minister's Office (PMO), which was intended to downgrade its status. The interference of the PMO in the different ministries was minimized. The importance of the cabinet was substantively restored, and its decisions were largely unanimous; the PM had become, once again, the first among equals. The system of 'joint responsibility' and 'prior cabinet clearance' was made functional.[24]

However, the PMO remained an office that was begun by Nehru. This legal status was not abolished; its new advisory role of initiating new policies, as stated by Tandon, continued. It did not return to its old role of providing only secretarial assistance. But its engagement with the party affairs, with which Indira Gandhi had empowered it, stopped.

In subsequent years, the functions of the PMO remained the same despite the change in prime ministers. Only minor changes were witnessed; one, for example, was the change of nomenclature of the PPS to secretary to principal secretary (PS). Nehru had the PPS, Shastri had the secretary, and from Indira Gandhi onwards it became the PS; Vajpayee created a new post of National Security Advisor, while Shastri and others had a media advisor. Then there was the principal advisor, economic advisor, and so on. The different PMs thus had their teams with bureaucratic ranks. This was not there in the British system, and Margaret Thatcher only initiated appointing advisors in 1979.

The second change became visible when coalition governments were formed as a result of coalition politics—this is when a single party is unable to secure a majority in the Lok Sabha and is forced to form a coalition government with other parties, either before the parliamentary election or as a result of it. The result was a change in the political position and status of the prime ministers, which was reflected in the status of the PMO. If the party of the PM was in absolute majority in the Lok Sabha, their PMO had a larger presence. But this is only a broad theorization. There are many minor variations, such as the personality of the prime ministers and their political weight within and outside the party, which would impact the acceptance of the PMO.

Also, within the PMO, the status of the principal secretaries, their acceptance among the officers while serving, and the mandate from the PM impact its domain, the most recent example being the distribution of the work between the PS, the National Security Advisor, and the principal advisor to the PM in the first Modi government.[25] But one fact has remained irreversible: since 1964, the PMO's role towards the PM has remained unchanged; from secretarial assistance to ensuring policy application, from policy formulation to intervention in the ministries, it has consistently advised the prime ministers.

PMO Bureaucracy

The procedure of working in the PMO is different compared to the other ministries. When the files are called for or received from different ministries, no notes are written on the files in the PMO, unlike the procedures in the other government departments. Rather, a new parallel file or a photocopy of the ministries' file is created; it is matched with the old file already kept in the PMO. This file that is kept in the PMO is called the ghost/shadow file, on which the decisions taken in the PMO are written.

Once the decision is taken, the original files of the ministries are returned with the directives and decisions written on them; if the PM's signature is required on the file before sending it to the president for his signature, it is processed accordingly, and a photocopy of it is put into the ghost file of the PMO. In this way, the PMO also acts as the office of record with an in-built institutional memory. But it may be added here for clarification that the office has no legal authority and accountability like the other departments of the ministries. The different sections in the PMO act for the sake of convenience and efficiency of its functioning, which is to assist the PM. The assistance includes offering information and advice required by him in the decision-making and its application. The officers cannot direct their counterparts in the ministries. The departments in the ministries and the cabinet secretariat are, legally, the supreme unit.

The different ministries of the government and the state of the union, apart from the ministries directly under the purview of the PM, are entrusted to different sections of the PMO for scrutiny, supervision and coordination, something that was once strongly contested by Patel against Nehru in 1947.

Authority and Domain Expansion

From time to time, different prime ministers have brought different agencies/departments under their direct purview. For example, Indira Gandhi brought the Department of Enforcement and the Department of Revenue Intelligence under the PMS, which were earlier part of the Ministry of Finance. Morarji Desai later returned these to the ministry. Similarly, the Intelligence Bureau (IB), Central Bureau of Investigation (CBI), Criminal Investigation Department (CID), and Research and Analysis Wing (R&AW) were brought within the fold of the cabinet secretariat; earlier, these departments were part of the Ministry of Home Affairs.

As the domain of the PM has expanded, so has the domain of the PMO in similar proportion. It has also simultaneously developed an institutional memory of being the office of record with five sections,[26] namely Economic and Social-I (E and S-I), Economic and Social-II (E and S-II), Political-I (Pol. I), Political-II

(Pol. II) and Not to Go Out (NGO), headed by a section officer. Each section has its assistants and section officers, and accordingly, the deputy secretaries, directors and joint secretaries.

But the PMO, as stated earlier, legally speaking, is not a department. It only provides secretarial assistance to the PM; it is just an office. Yet it is the most important office, as over the decades the nature of the government has become practically prime ministerial. Its extra-constitutional growth reflects the intents of the prime ministers and its acceptance in due time.

PMO Interference

It is well known that the PMS/PMO has been interfering in the functioning of the different departments of the ministries and administration, in general. The officers manning it call it coordination for efficient results. In Nehru's time, Mathai, the special assistant in the PMS, emerged as the key person in the 1950s, after the death of Patel. During Shastri's tenure, the mandate of the PMS was changed, making way for its emergence as the informal mini-government of the unelected babus. It also simultaneously became an informal secretariat. This, compounded by the creation of 'ghost files' of the different ministries under the direct command of the prime ministers, gave the babus in the PMS a taste of power. Over the course of time, it became a self-perpetuating system, leading to an informal subversion of the hierarchy of bureaucracy and collective functioning of the cabinet, resulting in the concentration of power in the PMS. Indira's PMS-PMH was known for running the government and the party. Similar was the case with the Rajiv Gandhi and the Rao governments.

The antidote to this subversion was the development of coalition governments, which acted as a political restraint on prime ministers through the coalition of parties forming the governments. A partial exception to it was the Vajpayee PMO, headed by Brajesh Mishra, who 'represented' Vajpayee as his authoritative voice. Gopal Krishna Gandhi called him 'one single lode stone charging the terrain and holding it' (the coalition government).[27] The prime ministers, and hence their PMOs, were restrained by the absence of the one-party rule, or rather by the in-built nature of the coalition governments.

Memoirs of the civil servants who worked in the PMO are reflections of their functioning at the time. In the Vajpayee era, for example, despite Vajpayee's commanding position, the coalition parties in the government formation felt empowered for 'bargaining better positions' due to the absence of a majority of the BJP in the Lok Sabha.[28] In such cases, prime ministers felt circumspect in choosing their ministers, allocating their portfolios, and determining and prioritizing the agenda of the government, as these were decided after negotiations with the coalitional parties. The ministers of the coalition parties preferred to choose their officers, which has now been stopped.

With the coming of the Modi government, this is now regulated by the Appointments Committee of the Cabinet (ACC). The babus and the PS to the ministers are thus restrained in their free run. The officers in the PMO, however, are usually not disturbed by the change of prime ministers. Even principal secretaries have had extended tenures with changing prime ministers. L.K. Jha and many others continued even with new prime ministers. It may be noted here that 'the principal secretary and private secretary serve the same term in office as their boss (the prime minister), unless sacked without notice... Vajpayee's clear instructions were that...all officers from the secretary down would remain. Vacancies would be filled in by normal means unless some specific expertise was required.'[29]

Principal Secretary

Over the decades, the PMO and the PS have developed overarching roles. The PS's role has become political and administrative, from suggesting the names of the ministers to be included in the council of ministers to representing the country on behalf of the PM; he also decides which file is to be submitted to the PM for his priority consideration. His emergence in such a role has been solely because of the individual nature of the person holding the post of PM. Except for this, there is no constitutionally-given inherent power of the PS.

Some of the prominent principal secretaries who changed the PMO are L.K. Jha, P.N. Haksar, P.C. Alexander and Brajesh Mishra. However, they were their masters' voice and also thought of 'ruling at a personal level'.[30] There is no doubt that prime ministers, from Nehru to Modi, need help to run the country, and a personal, informal rapport with the civil servants helps them. But rather than being dependent on the PMO, they could be equally assisted by the cabinet secretariat. The only constraint is that the cabinet secretariat is a formal organization to assist the executive in the formulation and application of the decisions taken by the government. The PMO has no such formal mandate except for assisting the prime ministers. Deve Gowda took the help of joint secretaries and directors to understand the issues. Narasimha Rao, on the other hand, sought help from the Department of Trade and Industry of Britain to streamline the functioning of his PMO.

Similarly, Nehru wrote to Attlee to understand the functioning of the British PMs.

Works on PMO

Different works on the PMS, primarily the memoirs of civil servants, adopt both structuralist and instrumentalist approaches to critique or justify its creation. But unfortunately most of these works are chapters or articles on the PMS reporting its broad functioning, lacking academic rigour in analysis. Even in the academic works, the focus is more on the cabinet, parliament, political parties or political and non-political biographies of the PM; the PMS remains a chapter.

The earliest works began to emerge in the 1970s, when civil servants started writing their memoirs after their retirement; Vidya Shankar's *My Reminiscences of Sardar Patel* (1974), S.S. Dharma Vira's *Memoirs of a Civil Servant* (1975), Khera's *The Central Executive* (1975), and M.O. Mathai's *Reminiscences of the Nehru Age* (1978) are some examples of the early works. Subsequently, many others have followed, the most recent being Shakti Sinha's *Vajpayee*. Meanwhile, there were correspondences which have been published; for example, Durga Das's edited *Sardar Patel's Correspondence* (1972). Academic books have also conducted intensive research on the functioning of the cabinet, PM and PMS, the most notable in this genre being Madhu Limaye's *Cabinet Governance in India* (1989) and V.A. Pai Panandiker and Ajay K. Mehra's *The Indian Cabinet* (1996). Among biographical works, the most recent publications are Vinay Sitapati's *Jugalbandi (2020)*, which is about Vajpayee and Advani.

In the biographical genre focused on prime ministers, there

are two kinds of works: one on individual prime ministers, such as S. Gopal on Nehru, C.P. Srivastava on Shastri (1995), Wajahat Habibullah on Rajiv Gandhi (2020), Shakti Sinha on Vajpayee (2020); the second on prime ministers in general, including Janardan Thakur's *All the Prime Minister's Men* (1977) and Neerja Chowdhury's *How Prime Ministers Decide* (2023).

Memoirs and biographical works gain more publicity and are controversial, while academic works remain confined to research, laying the foundation for further research, and have longer shelf lives. Some of the controversial memoirs of their times have been Mathai's *Reminiscences of the Nehru Age*, B.N. Tandon's *PMO Diary I,* and Sanjay Baru's *The Accidental Prime Minister: The Making and Unmaking of Manmohan Singh.* They brought into the public domain the inner functioning of the prime ministers, their strengths and weaknesses, and the details of their PMS.

But as stated earlier, rarely any book has questioned, let alone criticized, the extra-secretarial expansion of the powers of the PMS after 1964. What has been examined is the misuse of the PMS, or the growth of the PMH, as a parallel secretariat to the PMS, resulting in its marginalization. The marginalization of the cabinet secretariat by the PMS after 1964 is less discussed and rarely criticized, even though its growth has been uncalled for and extra-constitutional. The marginalization of the cabinet secretariat was symptomatic of a deep malaise that reflected the marginalization of the cabinet. In England, it's the cabinet secretariat that still acts as the fulcrum of administration, despite being more than 100 years old; it emerged in 1916, during the war years. The PMS only provides secretarial assistance to the PM; in 1964, PM Harold Wilson had only eight staff members. He wanted to 'increase it, but could add only one'. But, as mentioned earlier, the authors did not question the growth of the extra-secretarial role of the PMS after 1964, which they thought was inevitable or a necessity at the time. Srivastava has argued that the PMS was an innovation 'which could lead to some overlap with the functions of the Cabinet Secretariat.'[31]

Among the articles in research journals, three are notable: B.G. Deshmukh's 'Prime Minister's Office: We Cannot and Need not Do Without It'; another is R.R. Jha's 'Prime Minister's Office: The Fulcrum of Indian Administration'. Both the papers published in the *Indian Journal of Public Administration* profess the need and inevitability of the PMS. In fact, the captions of their papers reflect their views. However, another take is Karuna Singh's 'Prime Minister's Office: A Critical Analysis', published in the *Indian Journal of Political Science* as part of her doctoral work. She is one of the rare researchers who questioned the extra-secretarial expansion of the powers of the PMS, terming it 'a parallel government'; Deshmukh, Srivastava and others knew that the PMS 'has usurped the powers of the Cabinet Secretariat and actively interfered with the working of various Ministries and Departments,'[32] yet they advocated for it. They knew about the powers and functioning of the British cabinet secretariat, its position vis-à-vis the British PMS, and the role of the PMS towards the PM; yet they supported the transformation of the Indian PMS that was created in 1964. When the PMS was bypassed by the PMH, they had a problem; when Indira Gandhi engaged Haksar, the PS, in the party affairs, there was not even a murmur questioning the decision. Civil servants tend to enjoy the hierarchy and power relations: the higher their positions in the Warrant of Precedence, the better it is for them. The problem emerges when they are bypassed.

To sum up, in the past seven and half decades, there have been notable changes in the PMO: the rank of the PPS has been constantly upgraded, from the deputy secretary to the cabinet secretary to the rank of the cabinet minister; there has been the appointment of retired civil servants and the creation of the post of National Security Advisor (NSA). Till 1971, there was no retired officer in the PMS; the first retired officer to be appointed was P.N. Haksar. In 1998, the post of the NSA was created and also of the Economic Advisory Council (EAC). But the overall role of the PMS-PMO has remained intact, reflecting the arrival of the prime ministerial government, despite constitutionally being the cabinet form of government. While Nehru marginalized the cabinet, Shastri marginalized the cabinet secretariat. In the subsequent years, this remained unchanged. Only in the years of coalition governments was there a substantive restoration of the cabinet and its secretariat.

Congress Years

Jawaharlal Nehru

On 14 August 1947, Jawaharlal Nehru had an informal meeting with the cabinet secretary, H.M. Patel, and other officials to discuss the formation and role of the Prime Minister's Secretariat (PMS) and the cabinet secretariat. 'Nehru heard patiently the arguments why he should not have a high-powered (PM) Secretariat. He listened to the arguments carefully and also read Lord Ismay's letter'[1] that Patel had sought. It had an impact on Nehru. For the next seventeen years, the functioning of his PMS remained secretarial. He retained the cabinet secretariat as the fulcrum of the administration.

Lord Ismay, it must be stated here, was the chief of staff (advisor) to Lord Mountbatten, who brought him to India when he joined as the Viceroy in March 1947. H.M. Patel was also the PPS to Nehru in 1947, so appointed to link Nehru with the cabinet secretariat. The backdrop to this letter stated Nehru's desire to form a 'high-powered Secretariat under him, with which he [was to use to] swamp the Cabinet Secretariat.'[2] This desire was there from the beginning and it came to the fore when he joined the interim government and sought this PMS from Wavell. Wavell provided him with a few staff for his secretarial assistance, including H.M. Patel, the then joint secretary in the cabinet secretariat; but this was not what Nehru was asking for.

On the eve of Independence, his desire was once again ignited. When opposed by the officials, he finally relented.

The cabinet secretariat itself was created in 1945, modelled on the pattern of the same in the United Kingdom, to provide assistance to the EC and to the incoming Indian cabinet to run the government. The Viceroy's EC was then serviced by the Law Department, whose secretary was also the secretary of the council and whose work was to primarily to keep the records of the meetings. The new cabinet secretariat, headed by Eric Coates, the first cabinet secretary, had both civil and military wings; earlier, the military wing was a separate unit, known as the War Department and headed by the commander-in-chief, which was 'independent of civil government', enjoying a special status working directly under the Viceroy. The two wings of the government had skeleton contacts 'primarily through the officers of the Department'.

In the military wing of the new cabinet secretariat, 'a couple of military officers were included' for better civil-military coordination and to 'keep track of matters military'. Moreover, it was 'to ensure that the decisions taken by the EC were carried out by the various ministries.'[3.] Mountbatten had suggested seeking Ismay's opinion on the cabinet secretariat and the PMS, which was discussed informally with Nehru on 14 August 1947. It was to create an authoritative but informal view for the continuation of the cabinet secretariat, which had stood the test of time in England through the two World Wars. It was also to highlight the point that under the cabinet secretariat, the military would be tracked and function under the command of the civilian administration of the Cabinet government, as it operated in England. Subsequently, post 1947, the position of commander-in-chief was abolished for better civilian control; the War Department, which was 'independent of civilian government' in the colonial regime, was brought under the Ministry of Defence. Nehru then kept the PMS under the radar, using it only for secretarial work, while he used the cabinet secretariat, as envisaged in the British model, in an advisory role, to maintain close contact with the secretaries of the various ministries for the implementation of decisions and 'to ensure the smooth working of the government'.[4]

But after the death of H.M. Patel, Nehru began to marginalize the Cabinet. In fact, even when he was alive, the process was on. Patel, the first Indian cabinet secretary, presented a vivid description of the process: 'The PM (Nehru) himself has repeatedly taken decisions on his own in matters relating to the External Affairs Ministry, which is in his direct charge. A special Committee of the Cabinet for Foreign Affairs has been in existence almost from the beginning. All important matters, in particular all policy matters, have to be brought before this committee and its decisions have to be reported to the entire Cabinet. Time and again, however, decisions of the greatest importance have been taken and announced to the public without this committee being aware of them.'[5]

The cabinet form of government is 'presumed to act as one man on all questions relating to government policy and its implementation,'[6] which was adopted from the British model along with most of its conventions. In practice, however, 'quite significant differences have emerged' in India, while in the British system 'so far no significant dent has been made'.[7] The reason was that several cabinet ministers following Nehru began to bypass the cabinet. They used to obtain Nehru's concurrence and go ahead 'without waiting for the Cabinet's approval'.[8] Contrary to this, Sardar Patel strictly adhered to the procedures. He kept his 'colleagues informed' and obtained 'the approval of the Cabinet to the terms of the settlement with every ruler', even though in the state ministry, negotiations had to be carried on with a large number of princely states with considerable variations in the treaty arrangements.[9] Nehru, on the other hand, had remarked in a cabinet meeting that 'Cabinet or no Cabinet, so long as I am the Prime Minister I will carry out my policy.'[10] It was not an angry, impulsive reaction by the PM. It was his psychology that had been visible since the day he joined the government. The second dent was Nehru's interference with the functioning of the ministries; if he did not like any particular act,[11] instead of discussing the matter in the cabinet and letting the cabinet make a decision after the concerned minister's explanation, he would cut short the process and bypass the cabinet. As a consequence, a precedent was set that impacted the position and functioning of the cabinet over time and culminated in the imposition of the Emergency by Indira Gandhi, without the cabinet's prior approval.

Imitating Nehru, different ministers began to interfere with the routine functioning of their ministries by bypassing their secretaries and other procedures. V.K. Krishna Menon, for example, interfered with the routine functioning of the armed forces, which was one of the serious reasons for the debacle in the 1962 war with China. This interference had cascading effects over time, right down to the lowest rung in the hierarchy. Menon played favourites that created 'cliques within the forces', failing to interpret 'the services' professional point of view' that led to a wrong military assessment of the strength of the Chinese army[12] and its military ability 'to deter anyone from attacking it'.

Also, the marginalization of the cabinet led to the

marginalization of the cabinet secretariat and the emergence of the PMS as an informal substitute for the secretariat after the 1962 Sino–Indian War. This was when Shastri was brought back into the cabinet in January 1964 as a minister without a portfolio, following his resignation in 1963 under the Kamaraj Plan. The decline of the cabinet secretariat in India was 'influenced by the way the cabinet system had worked'. In England, on the contrary, the secretariat still plays a significant advisory role to the PM and the other cabinet ministers. The cabinet's advice is sought for appointment to various posts, and it 'irons out inter-departmental differences', besides being the official record keeper of the files.

In India, it plays a passive role despite being designated to play an essential role in the functioning of the government. In 1947, Dharma Vira, the then cabinet secretary, argued that it was 'in the process of evolution as the lines of demarcation of responsibility had not been settled due to the problems of partition.' H.M. Patel, on the other hand, felt that the 'Cabinet Secretaries themselves tended to take a much less dynamic view of their position.'[13]

There were two other factors which were more damaging: one, cabinet ministers rarely stood up to Nehru for his un-cabinet-like functioning; second, Nehru maintained, from the very beginning, a prime ministerial form of government that subsequently resulted in the emergence of the PMS as a 'miniature government', transforming itself from the status of the personal secretarial office. The process of strengthening the PMS began during the last years of Nehru's tenure and took a formal shape when Shastri took over as the PM. What Nehru did through the stature of his persona without creating a leviathan in the form of the PMS, Shastri did through the PMS by transforming its role.

marginalisation of the cabinet secretariat and the emergence of the PMS as an informal substitute for the secretariat after the 1962 Sino-Indian War—this was when Shastri was brought back into the cabinet in January 1964 as a minister without a portfolio, following his resignation in 1963 under the Kamaraj Plan. The decline of the cabinet secretariat in India was influenced by the [illegible] of the cabinet system that worked in England, and the secretariat still plays a significant advisory role to the PM and the other cabinet ministers, the cabinet's advisers [illegible] appointment to various posts, and [illegible] inter-departmental differences, besides being the official record keeper of the [illegible]

In India, it plays a passive role despite being designed to play an essential role in the functioning of the government. In 1967, Dharma Vira, the then cabinet secretary, argued that it was in the process of evolution as the lines of demarcation of responsibility had not been settled due to the [illegible] partition. H.M. Patel, on the other hand, felt that the cabinet secretaries themselves tended to take a much less dynamic view of their position.

The instrument of the PMS, however, also acquired self-perpetuating administrative powers over the course of time. Nehru wanted this instrument, designed in 1947, to swap every other organ of the administration, but he had to forego this desire. Much later, Brecher wrote about the PMS, citing L.K. Jha, the Secretary to the PM, that the PMS was going to emerge as a leviathan in the future. Srivastava, the political biographer of Shastri, who was also his private secretary in the PMS, knew Shastri since the 1950s; however, he considered this change in the PMS as a 'change in nomenclature' as well as an 'innovation which could lead to some overlap with the functions of the cabinet secretariat.'[18] How wrong he was, was proved well by the subsequent developments.

As prime ministers, both Nehru and Shastri had different styles of functioning, but their objectives were similar—a command over the cabinet. Nehru was overtly interfering by nature, a habit from his early years. Even when he was not the president of the Congress, he behaved as if he were. Subhash Bose was often annoyed at this habit.[19] During cabinet meetings, Nehru would sum up the discussion as per his line of thinking, which would then become the decision of the cabinet, despite the divergent views expressed by different ministers. He posited himself as the cabinet's representative; his summing up created an impression that his decision or view was the consensus of the cabinet.

Shastri, on the other hand, maintained a soft external demeanour, listening to every view; but he too summed up discussions in Nehru's style, making his view the policy or the final word of the cabinet. As part of Nehru's cabinet, he had closely observed the functioning of the cabinet and its secretariat and Nehru himself. He substituted the commanding-domineering style of Nehru with patience by listening to divergent views without changing his objective of desiring command over the cabinet. The 'gaps' in the functioning of ministries and ministers were taken care of by his PMS, which was given a new role. Many of his decisions were taken in consultation with civil servants without any prior discussion with ministers and the cabinet. Indira Gandhi had expressed it categorically that way.[20] Vesting the PMS with new powers and trusting it indeed had their consequences, which were visible in Kutch in 1965 and subsequently in the post-war Tashkent Agreement. India ceded ten per cent of its territory in the Rann of Kutch and returned key posts in Kashmir, which the Indian Army had besieged during the war with Pakistan in 1965. Even the decision to refer the Kutch dispute to the international tribunal was taken by civil servants.[21]

What Nehru did to the cabinet because of his intrinsic nature, corroborated by examples, became a regular feature in due course; Shastri did it subtly but systemically, by enacting laws. Both wanted complete control over their cabinets, for which they adopted different methods as per their individual traits and the requirements of the situations in which they were placed. Shastri's actions were more damaging, as they were systemic, as observed by T.P. Singh. N.K. Singh, another civil servant, too observed: 'That the primacy of the position of the Cabinet Secretary emanated from his being the last person to tender any advice to the PM and that from here onwards as his secretary, L.K. Jha's note would be the last one to be read by the PM. This made a qualitative and structural difference in the hierarchy of the civil service establishment.'[22] This structural change also increased the strength of the staff in the PMS. Between 1965 and 1966, it swelled to 229–35, which had been approximately

Shastri, provides a vivid description of the matter.[26] Mackintosh provides a vivid account of the composition and functioning of the British PMS. When PM Wilson inducted Marcia Williams to look after the correspondence of his constituency, there was serious opposition to her entry till her role was defined.[27] This was an innovation of the time in the British PMS. Subsequently, the post became its acceptable part. In comparison, Shastri's PMS (or even Nehru's PMS) was numerically large and administratively powerful. Since Shastri's tenure as the PM was cut short, the impact of the PMS was not as glaringly visible as it became during the Indira Gandhi years. Also, Shastri's behaviour towards civil servants and the cabinet, apparently in contrast to that of Nehru and Indira, managed to cover up the emerging phantom role of the PMS as a miniature government, which it became during Indira's tenure.

After Shastri's death, Indira Gandhi was made the PM for the sheer reason that she would be under the control of the Congress syndicate. It was to checkmate Morarji Desai. The same policy had been applied while selecting Shastri to checkmate Morarji Desai after Nehru's death. When Shastri was made the PM, Kamaraj was the Congress president. Despite his marginalization by Shastri, he did not learn the lesson. While selecting Indira Gandhi, Shastri, after becoming the PM, did not even consult Kamaraj in the cabinet's formation. In fact, Kamaraj was kept waiting in an adjoining room while Shastri along with his civil servants and son-in-law finalized the list of cabinet ministers. Once it was finalized, Kamaraj was merely shown the list. Similarly, when Indira Gandhi became the PM, he was again shown the door. This time, the party was split. Kamaraj himself lost the election in 1967. Earlier, the Kamaraj Plan had been engineered to facilitate the departure of senior ministers in the Nehru cabinet, clearing the way for Shastri as the future PM. Nehru trusted Shastri, who had been working with him since the 1920s. He believed that Shastri would take care of Indira Gandhi, who was inducted into his cabinet at the fourth rank in the warrant of precedence.

The purpose of the analogy presented here is to contend that both the prime ministers who succeeded Nehru had learnt their respective functioning styles from him. He was also responsible for building his political family dynasty. Indira Gandhi was made the president of the Congress in 1959 despite opposition from Govind Ballabh Pant. It was thought that the Congress presidency would facilitate her prime ministership in the future, as Nehru himself was brought closer to the prime ministership by Mahatma Gandhi through the Congress presidency. In fact, it was Motilal Nehru who had written to Gandhi, suggesting to him that he make Jawaharlal Nehru the president of the Congress after the end of his tenure.

Such developments were detrimental to the collective functioning of the cabinet and impacted the position of the cabinet secretariat and fostered the PMS. In Nehru's PMS, there were 150 staff members, including 12 gazetted officers, which increased to 200 by the time Shastri took over two years later. Since L.K. Jha, the secretary in the PMS, and Dharam Vira, the cabinet secretary, were friends, the conflict over jurisdiction was sorted out; yet Dharam Vira did not like this new role of the PMS, or its encroachment into the domain of the cabinet secretariat.

When Indira Gandhi took over the prime ministership on 29 January 1966, she continued with L.K. Jha for a year before replacing him with P.N. Haksar. Haksar has been blamed, along with Indira Gandhi, for destroying the autonomy of government departments. He completed the task, as was visualized by Nehru

[illegible] democratic traditions? Or is it the [illegible] of the [illegible] impositions of the British [illegible] which is more urban industrial along with a [illegible] of suffrage that impacts the nature of the cabinet and the parties?

In 1964, when PM Wilson wanted additional help in his PMS to look after the correspondence of his constituency, there was reluctance from the staff. The PM had to clarify and demarcate the role of the new staff to avoid the friction. In comparison, in India, Shastri restructured the whole PMS in 1964 with a new mandate without any resistance which subsequently became the benchmark of administration, including its replication in the states as the Chief Minister's Secretariat/Chief Minister's Office (CMS/CMO).

Under his boss Indira Gandhi, Haksar took the functioning of the PMS to a new level, which had been initiated by Shastri while looking after the cabinet secretariat as a minister with no portfolio from January to May 1964. During Nehru's time, the PMS was given the status of a department under the Allocation of Business Rules 1947 (AOB), while the Cabinet Secretariat was given the [illegible] status of the Secretariat of the Council of Ministers. Nehru, like Viceroy Wellington, also initiated the practice of taking his PS in cabinet meetings which was strongly opposed by [illegible]. Due to this opposition, the PMS was stopped from attending the meetings. Shastri, on the advice of L.K. Jha, approved his [illegible] presence in the cabinet meeting which [illegible] [illegible] the cabinet secretary according to the warrant of precedence.

The [illegible] of the PMS was officially designated to provide secretarial assistance to the PM through a new insertion in the AOB members have more evolved democratic traditions? Or is it due to structural differences in terms of the social composition of the British electorate, which is more urban-industrial, along with a revolutionary tradition of suffrage, that impacts the nature of the cabinet and the parties?

In 1964, when PM Wilson wanted additional help in his PMS to look after the correspondence of his constituency, there was resistance from the staff. The PM had to clarify and demarcate the role of the new staff to end the friction. In comparison, in India, Shastri restructured the whole PMS in 1964 with a new mandate without any resistance, which subsequently became the benchmark of administration, including its replication in the states as the Chief Minister's Secretariat/Chief Minister's Office (CMS/CMO).

Under his boss Indira Gandhi, Haksar took the functioning of the PMS to a new low, which had been initiated by Shastri while looking after the cabinet secretariat as a minister without a portfolio from January to May 1964. During Nehru's time, the PMS was given the status of a department under the Allocation of Business Rules 1961 (AOB), while the cabinet secretariat was given the legal status of the Secretariat of the Council of Ministers.[34] Nehru, like Viceroy Willingdon, also initiated the practice of taking his PPS to cabinet meetings, which was strongly opposed by Patel. Due to this opposition, the PPS was stopped from attending the meetings. Shastri, on the advice of L.K. Jha, approved his official presence in the cabinet meeting which was also made equal to the cabinet secretary, according to the warrant of precedence.

The role of the PMS was officially designated to provide secretarial assistance to the PM through a new insertion in the AOB.

Such changes initiated by Nehru, structurally changed by Shastri, and applied in a full-blown form by Indira Gandhi permanently eroded the primacy of the cabinet secretariat in practice, which was replicated in the CMS. Officially, the cabinet secretariat is still the custodian of administration; in praxis, however, it's the PMS. For when the cabinet itself lost its efficacy during the Nehru years, when the ministers bypassed the procedures with his consultation, it was inevitable that its custodian, the cabinet secretariat, would lose its importance. Indira Gandhi and Rajiv Gandhi made the cabinet leadership redundant.

The worst part was that even the PMS was unaware of many administrative aspects, which the Prime Minister's House (PMH) regulated during the respective tenures of these prime ministers. Even during Nehru's regime, his special assistant Mathai became an important functionary in the PMH after the death of Patel. During Shastri's regime, when L.K. Jha's rank became equal to the cabinet secretary, T.P. Singh, his ICS batchmate, sarcastically remarked while congratulating him on his official elevation that he had permanently destroyed the supremacy of the cabinet secretariat.

Then came the PMH. PM Indira Gandhi's son Sanjay Gandhi started '...his interference in administration and government... with his Maruti project. How his mother allowed him to misuse her office and power has been recorded (by many)... To help him, the prime minister attached one of her assistants to him and Sanjay's orders and wishes were conveyed to different ministries and offices through this assistant... Indira Gandhi used to send her ministers and senior officials to Sanjay for order[s],'[35] who met him in the PMH, reported about their work and sought his orders. It resulted in numerous appointments in the government

the [illegible] had begun; the [illegible] [illegible] of [illegible] or systemic [illegible] was yet to happen. What was instinctive in Nehru's personality traits was [illegible] at a systemic level by Indira Gandhi. The grassroots cadres and the legislators were no longer the determinants in ticket distribution or in elections to party posts. The absence of a credible alternative party to the Congress and other emerging regional parties with their own dynamics facilitated its perpetuation. The electorate voted for the leaders who belonged to their castes and religions in their constituencies.

The [illegible] of the emergence of the Nehru dynasty was replicated by other parties and within the Congress. The monopoly of political power by the Congress and by the Nehru dynasty had disastrous consequences for the functioning of the cabinet system. Parties became instruments to serve the dynasties. While the electorate voted for the alternative dynastic leadership, the party was no longer a critical regulator and determinant; the cabinet became a legal formality.

By 1977, the cabinet and the party had their epitaphs written large on their tombstones. The return of Indira Gandhi in 1980 and the [illegible] of Rajiv Gandhi in 1984 reinforced the epitaphs. During her second term, Indira Gandhi began to upset the [illegible] of informal advisers and the ministers. [illegible] began to be routed through her PS, [illegible], the PMO had now become a shadow cabinet.

This resulted in a behavioural change in the functioning of the civil servants in the PMO, who began to [illegible] power relations with their colleagues in the ministries. The joint secretary, or even deputy secretaries would only deal with the [illegible] or secretaries of other departments and would zealously guard their the dent had begun; the Kamaraj Plan was symptomatic of it. But this kind of systemic destruction was yet to happen. What was instinctive in Nehru's personality traits was actuated at a systemic level by Indira Gandhi. The grassroots cadres and the legislators were no longer the determinants in ticket distribution or in elections for party posts. The absence of a credible alternative party to the Congress and other emerging regional parties with their own dynasties facilitated its perpetuation. The electorate voted for the leaders who belonged to their castes and religions in their constituencies.

The form of the emergence of the Nehru dynasty was replicated by other parties and within the Congress. The monopoly of political power by the Congress and by the Nehru dynasty had disastrous consequences for the functioning of the cabinet system. Parties became instruments to serve the dynasties. While the electorate voted for the alternative dynastic leadership, the party was no longer a critical mediator and determinant; the cabinet became a legal formality.

By 1977, the cabinet and the party had their epitaphs written large on their tombstones. The return of Indira Gandhi in 1980 and the victory of Rajiv Gandhi in 1984 reinforced the epitaphs. During her second term, Indira Gandhi began to meet the secretaries of different ministries and the ministers' files began to be routed through her PS, P.C. Alexander. The PMO had now become a shadow cabinet.

This resulted in a behavioural change in the functioning of the civil servants in the PMO, who began to enjoy new power relations with their colleagues in the ministries. 'The Joint Secretary or even deputy secretaries would only deal with the ministries or secretaries of other departments and would zealously guard their authority.'[39] The change in nomenclature, from PMS to PMO, by the Morarji Desai government did not change the power relation in the long run. The subsequent PMOs of Indira Gandhi and Rajiv Gandhi reflected this amply.

Rajiv Gandhi

After the death of his mother, Rajiv Gandhi was sworn in as the next PM on 31 October 1984. Indira Gandhi's PS, P.C. Alexander, continued for a year and was subsequently replaced by Sarla Grewal, followed by B.G. Deshmukh. The PMO was now flooded with advisers with high visibility, such as Mani Shankar Aiyer, Montek Singh Ahluwalia, Ronen Sen, Sam Pitroda, G.K. Arora, G. Parthasarathy, and R. Vasudavan, who were also partly substituting the role of the Planning Commission in the formulation of the Eighth Plan. Rajiv Gandhi collaborated with them, at least during the initial months, but subsequently did say that he desired to restore the cabinet system and that his style of functioning was different from that of his mother. He argued that he let ministers deal with the issues of their ministries 'entirely on their own', and never interfered. But he did accept that certain issues required clearance from the PMO, as 'it has to go through a system.'[40] The response from the ministers, however, when journalists asked about any issues, would always be that the file had 'gone to the PMO for clearance.'[41] This might have been a way to evade answering and to deflect the issue of the non-performance of their ministries. Indeed, since the 1950s some ministers had been running their ministries like their own fiefdoms, which became more visible during PM Manmohan Singh's tenure. While during Rajiv Gandhi's time this occurred in consultation with the PM, during Manmohan Singh's tenure it was the result of coalition politics.

The NAC, headed by Sonia Gandhi, had become another parallel cabinet of unelected 'activist-advisors' and was another reason for the evasive responses given by the ministers. The NAC itself was like the PMH, another innovation. Some of the officers of the PMS—for example, Pulok Chatterjee, the joint secretary in the PMS—reported to the chairperson of the NAC. It was similar to the situation when the ministers and the civil servants were reporting to Sanjay Gandhi during Indira Gandhi's tenure.

Rajiv Gandhi ran the government like a 'monarch'; he had no idea about the functioning of the cabinet.[42] What he saw upon his entry into politics after Sanjay Gandhi's death was his mother's style of running the government. And he was well aware of the critics' arguments against Indira Gandhi's style. Therefore, he attempted to reinforce the argument in an interview that he wanted to restore the functioning of the cabinet. In practice, the case was just the opposite. The decision-making process at the time for the appointment of civil servants, governors, chief ministers, cabinet ministers and other roles is laid out in R.D. Pradhan's memoir. Pradhan's appointment as the home secretary as well as Arjun Singh's appointment as the chief minister of Madhya Pradesh and as the governor of Punjab the following day were indicative of the malaise.[43]

Rajiv Gandhi's unprecedented victory in the history of the Lok Sabha elections in independent India might have prompted illusionary thinking in him about the cabinet being comparable to the advisors to American presidencies. However, that was not the case. In India, the members of the cabinet had reduced themselves to a pathetic status. They were neither aides nor advisors in the style of the American presidency; nor were they cabinet ministers in the British tradition, which had a consequential impact on the cabinet system. The cabinet secretariat and its secretary never got their official due as advisors, a role which was in practice till Nehru's time despite the decline of the cabinet. Their position was taken over by the PMS-PMO, which was unofficially performing the task of the cabinet through the secretaries of the various ministries. This had a gradual cascading effect on the functioning of the governments and the civil services in the states.

Fortunately, the chief secretaries and the cabinet ministers in the states still carry more weight, as chief ministers themselves have been reduced to the status of pigmies. Chosen in Delhi, rather than by the legislators of the state assemblies, most of the chief ministers do not command the majority support of their legislators. Many such developments were initiated by Nehru. For example, he blessed the Kamaraj Plan, which visualized the resignation of senior cabinet ministers and chief ministers to set them to work for the party so as to ensure that Morarji Desai and others were kept out of the line of succession for the PM's post,[44] facilitating Shastri's and Indira Gandhi's rise to power. Nehru had faith in Shastri that he would take care of Indira Gandhi, since the two had been working together since the 1920s and he had observed Shastri closely for decades. He had earlier made his daughter the Congress president, who then recommended the dismissal of the newly elected government of Kerala. It was through the presidency of the Congress that Nehru wanted Indira to step into the role of PM. After all, it was through the presidency of the Congress that Mahatma Gandhi had brought him to the post of PM.

Rajiv Gandhi inherited his mother's legacy despite 'the differences in their leadership styles and approaches to the challenges faced by the country.'[45] Rajiv appointed three elected members of parliament, Arun Singh, Ahmad Patel and Oscar Fernandes, as parliamentary secretaries in the PMO 'to ensure that the political responsibilities that had been assigned to [P.C.] Alexander [his PS] were dealt with by political advisors. This would ensure that the PMO does not remain the administrative leviathan that it was seen as having become'.[46] Alexander had earlier been entrusted by Indira Gandhi to deal with all issues, not only government matters but also political and party matters,[47] much as Haksar was earlier entrusted. Rajiv's experiment with his political advisors in the PMO 'failed', as Wajahat Habibullah would remark later. His very objective of simplifying the PMO failed. The government became more centred on the PMO 'more than it had ever done under his mother.'

What developed as a result of this approach and objective was massive staffing and expanded layouts, along with the growth of computerization. The National Informatics Centre (NIC) was tasked with linking the PMO with the ministries, which became the 'benchmark' and the 'principal tool of work' that accelerated communication in the government. The mainframe of the computer was housed in the basement of the South Block of Central Secretariat. Rajiv Gandhi's office, including the chairs, was also designed and modernized. The PM office chairs and the visitors' chairs were made equal in size, the carpet was cleaned, the building was renovated, and even the entrance to the PMO was changed. Now the staff had better, more comfortable, chambers. This layout has remained almost unchanged till date.

Rajiv Gandhi viewed civil servants as facilitators in the government's delivery mechanisms, given their wide-ranging field experiences to deliver products, resources and services to citizens. The modernization of his office and ministries with technology was intended for this objective. He was aware that one of the important reasons for the failure of past governments had been bureaucratic hurdles, which could be transcended through the transparency brought about by computers to be handled by experts. Montek Singh Ahluwalia, Mani Shankar Aiyar and others were brought into the PMO to overhaul the structure of the administration and to bring in new methods of governance. The matter was discussed in 1990 by the Committee of Secretaries, but with the coming of the new government headed by V.P. Singh, it was no longer a priority and was relegated to the background.

Unlike his mother, Rajiv Gandhi would participate in official discussions with 'frequent interjections' and 'provocative comments' to elicit creative ideas from civil servants and others. Indira Gandhi, on the contrary, would listen, speak little, 'mull over the suggestions', and 'conclude the meeting with her assessment'. This conclusion used to be her order. This was also the style of Nehru and Shastri, with minor differences. They summed up even the cabinet meetings with their own assessments and conclusions. The tragedy was that in most of the cabinet meetings, and even otherwise, particularly during the Indira years, rarely would there be any open discussion, nor would anyone open their mouth.

Madhu Limaye remarked that such cabinet ministers were 'spineless', which lengthened their ministerial longevity but damaged institutions and the system, leading to the growth of the prime ministerial office with its own external and internal fallouts. Rajiv Gandhi faced the brunt of such characters during his tenure as the PM. One of his cabinet ministers, Arun Nehru, was instrumental in the unlocking of the Ayodhya Temple. But Rajiv Gandhi was unaware of it till it was executed by the then UP chief minister Vir Bhadra Singh, whose appointment was facilitated by Arun Nehru. Vir Bhadra Singh didn't confirm the decision with Rajiv Gandhi, thinking that the 'suggestion' of Arun Nehru[48] was the order of the PM. Subsequently, once the PM knew about it, he dropped Arun Nehru from the cabinet. But this was not a solution to the systemic malaise that had crept into the cabinet since the Nehru days. The immediate fallout of Arun Nehru's suggestion was the historical trajectory which began to unfold in relation to Ayodhya in Indian politics that led to the emergence of the BJP.

One of the reasons for the dominance of the PMO was a disconnect between the PM and the citizens, who were less involved in policymaking. The more the 'rootless' experts and bureaucrats in policymaking, the greater became the disconnect. The application of policies that are top-driven results in a gap between the priorities and requirements of the masses and the services delivered to them. The worst effect of this kind, for example, was the Padma Shri being awarded to the elite; the same was also visible in the receivers of the grants of awards, as the rural poor working without media hype were inadequately awarded. The ideas of development and the drivers of growth were the 'experts' and their policies, which were applied by the PMO through the ministries. It became a PM-led and -driven approach to policies which the ministries and the cabinet applied. However, this is not to deny some of the credible policies and roles of the ministries in the development process.

The electoral victory of the parties in the elections determines the nature of the government. If the electorate votes for the parties' prime ministerial candidates, the nature of the government will be prime ministerial, and if the electorate votes for the party or the candidates in their constituencies, the probability of the formation of a cabinet government increases. That's how the history of electoral politics in India has been since 1952. Marginalizing grassroots leaders began with the Kamaraj Plan during the Nehru years; marginalizing the party began with the Indira Gandhi regime. This virus also gripped many other parties and over time resulted in the disconnect between the parties and the electorate, and even made the parties dependent on dynasties to come to power. Once prime ministers from dynasties took over, the PMO became an instrument of governance. That's exactly what happened with Rajiv Gandhi.

P.V. Narasimha Rao

After the death of Rajiv Gandhi, the Congress emerged as the single largest party, helped by the sympathy vote since Gandhi was assassinated while electioneering. The question then became who would be the next PM. Narasimha Rao was the second name suggested by Haksar and Satish Sharma for the sheer reason that he had no political base of his own, was inoffensive, and would be loyal to the family. The family would remain the power centre. The first name was Shankar Dayal Sharma, who refused to assume the mantle of prime ministership.

Once he became the PM, Rao chose Amar Nath Varma as his PS in the PMO and Raman Damodaran as his private secretary. Varma was retired but was working as a member secretary in the Planning Commission. Naresh Chandra was then made the cabinet secretary, Montek Singh and Jairam Ramesh from Rajiv Gandhi's PMO were retained, and J.N. Dixit was brought in as the Foreign Secretary.

The focus of the PMO was on the liberalization of the economy. Accordingly, in the style of the Indira Gandhi-Rajiv Gandhi tradition, the PMO, while keeping a low profile, ran the government by overcoming bureaucratic hurdles. Deshmukh recalled years later that 'the PMO was often definitely interfering with the normal governmental machinery, if not riding roughshod over it.'[49] It was a single-party government but had no majority. Rao ran the government without a majority in the Lok Sabha during the initial years. His low profile and inoffensive persona did not create hiccups. But most importantly, after Rajiv Gandhi's assassination, the other parties were not in a position to face the electorate so soon, lest they be swept away by the sympathy vote. Rao, therefore, ran the government comfortably during the initial months despite initiating the liberalization measures radically. He faced rebellion and questions within his party and from outside, but an engineered defection from other parties in the Lok Sabha secured a majority for him, which kept him in the safe zone.

When the Babri structure was demolished, Rao was at his official residence, keeping in constant touch with his cabinet secretary and home secretary to monitor the developments in Ayodhya. The administration was in constant touch with the UP government, asking it to restrain the *kar sevaks*, who were kept under control till noon. At 12.15 p.m., the demolition began; the paramilitary forces moved in to restrain the kar sevaks but they had no orders from the local administration; they were under strict orders not to fire on the kar sevaks in any case. By 2.30 p.m., the domes were demolished.

The demolition led to political and religious mayhem in the subsequent months. The Congress lost the confidence of the Muslims, and Rao was blamed for it. But he survived and ran the government for the next four years. A few days before he died at AIIMS, Delhi, Sonia Gandhi went to meet him. She stayed there from 10.30 p.m. to 2.30 a.m. Rao had told her, 'Why should I be blamed for something I have not done?' And he was right. He was promised by Shekhawat, Advani and Singhal that the structure would remain intact. Even for them, the fall of the domes was a shock; it was an unexpected event. The first breach of the security cordon was by a teenage boy who climbed the dome around 12.15 p.m. after jumping over the fence. As he began to chip away at the dome, within minutes the others followed, and by 2.30 p.m. all the domes had been demolished.

What had failed the government was the lack of intelligence inputs and/or their poor judgement. A day before the demolition, shovels, hammers and similar instruments had vanished from the local market shops. Also, the leaders had thought that the crowd would do no such thing. They had not anticipated it; nor were they aware of it. What was happening among the foot soldiers was not known to them. In the cabinet meetings held before the demolition, no one supported the imposition of President's rule, for it could not be imposed based on anticipation. In the evening, after the fall of the domes, the UP chief minister resigned, and when the central government's cabinet meeting was called for, a recommendation for initiating the President's rule was sent to the President. Rao's opponents, however, began their back-biting within the party once the live streaming of the demolition was on, charging him that he was part of a deliberate design. The whole thing was part of malicious propaganda. Yet his steely resolve, political experience, manoeuvrability and strong network kept his government running for the next four years.

While Manmohan Singh ran the liberalization course in tandem with Varma, the PS, who was looking after the industrial policy on behalf of Rao and also holding the industrial portfolio, manoeuvred key political developments; Rajiv Gandhi lacked this ability to navigate. Rao's provincial experiences came to good use in managing the contradictions. It was not that Rao's economic measures were unprecedented. During the initial years of his tenure, Rajiv Gandhi had actuated some piecemeal initiatives. But Rao changed their course consistently and systematically. His PMO and PS were the 'point man on economic reforms'.[50] Every Thursday, Varma would hold lunch in his South Block office for key civil servants related to different ministries actuating reforms, while he chalked out the details with them and sent them 'to the Cabinet for final approval'; this continued for five years.[51]

Rao also left an imprint on foreign policy, which needed a complete reorientation with the fall of the Soviet Union and the coming up of the liberalization measures. The country required quick and massive investments, for which ambassadors with a vision and market orientation were appointed. Countries that were economic powerhouses were cultivated. During the five years that he was the PM, India began to emerge as the next powerhouse. He had unleashed an engine of growth.

He remained the president of the party. When it was suggested that Sonia Gandhi become the president, he reported that he was not interested in creating two power centres, which prophetically emerged during Manmohan Singh's time. In fact while it seemed like two power centres, in reality there was only one: Sonia Gandhi. Rao manoeuvred successfully to avoid such a situation. He used to meet Sonia Gandhi but would keep the power to himself. The best proof of this was when he dropped M.L. Fotedar from the cabinet in the subsequent reshuffle; Fotedare had shouted at Rao in the cabinet meeting in the wake of the Babri fall. Rao also shifted Sharad Pawar to Mumbai as the Maharashtra chief minister. So he was on his own from the time of assuming charge as PM. He was no longer the same Rao who had been nominated and removed from chief ministership by Indira Gandhi in the 1970s.

Manmohan Singh

In 2004, power once again beckoned Sonia Gandhi. This time she nominated Manmohan Singh as the PM of India while she remained the party president. The idea was to 'let him run the routine affairs of the government while retaining the power of the government through the PMO, keeping the policy-making through the National Advisory Council, and the party through its presidency.' It was once again for the same reason: loyalty to the family had propelled her to nominate Manmohan Singh. She had inherited this legacy from her mother-in-law, who had substantively facilitated the destruction of inner-party democracy and weakened the collective functioning of the cabinet. Sonia's political experiences of the past decade had also made her wiser.

Manmohan Singh had once confessed to Sanjay Baru, his press secretary, that 'there cannot be two centres of power... I have to accept that the Party President is the centre of power.'[52] He knew he was answerable to Sonia Gandhi. Rao, once the PM, had not accepted this proposition. Manmohan, on the contrary, remained subservient; his decades of experience of working in the government had perhaps brought an attitudinal change.

It also helped him in his rise in the hierarchy. M.O. Mathai, R.K. Dhawan and Vincent George, in that order, all enjoyed power while being with Nehru, Indira Gandhi, Rajiv Gandhi and Sonia Gandhi, respectively. Manmohan Singh also remained loyal to the family, resulting in his nomination as the PM. But his loyalty had a catastrophic impact on the functioning of the government. He had to function with the given ministers and officers. They were mostly chosen by Sonia Gandhi or the presidents of the supporting parties.

In comparison, Rao had been in a far better position. In Manmohan's case, the power centre was Sonia Gandhi, the party president and the chairperson of the NAC, substantively impacting the running of the government. In fact, to the ministers she was the 'government'. Manmohan Singh did not have the last word even in the appointment of key officers. 'The Congress core group that met every Friday evening at 7 Race Course Road (RCR), became the effective management board of the party and the government,'[53] replacing, in practice, the Cabinet Committee on Political Affairs (CCPA). It led to the wilful absence of cabinet ministers from cabinet meetings. The PM had to go for pre-cabinet consultations with senior ministers to secure the passage of enlisted items on the agenda in formal cabinet meetings.

The other mechanism was the empowered group of ministers (EGOMs) who took decisions on behalf of the cabinet, which were then ratified by the cabinet. These decisions were not sent for pre-approval to the PMO, which, according to Sanjay Baru, undermined the authority of the PM.[54] But for democracy and the cabinet government, the process led to the most democratically taken decisions by informed ministers, which was akin to the functioning of the British cabinet. The only problem was that such a situation had emerged out of compulsions in which Manmohan Singh was helpless. It was not the PM but Sonia Gandhi who was running the government; she had no governmental responsibility but was the determinant factor in the functioning of the government; the PM had the responsibility but without any political authority. The decisions of the NAC were supreme; this was communicated by Pulok Chatterjee, the then joint secretary and later PS in the PMO. The most important among such decisions was the application of the National Common Minimum Programme (NCMP), in which all the concerned ministries were very efficient.

The PMO had three key aides: T.K.A. Nair, the PS, J.N. Dixit, the National Security Advisor (NSA), and M.K. Narayanan, the special advisor for internal security. While the PS coordinated with the PM, secretaries and ministers, the NSA coordinated with the service chiefs as well as the ministries of nuclear strategy, atomic energy, defence and external affairs. Internal security, usually coordinated by the NSA, was coordinated by Narayanan in this instance. Initially the appointment of multiple advisors led to conflicts, which were subsequently resolved through an office order distributing work to each of the three advisors. Then there were complaints from the ministers that there were interferences in their ministries caused by the PMO. The three officers had the rank of Minister of State (MoS), which was a novelty. Such novelties, however, had been taking place under the Congress regimes since Nehru, who had brought Shastri into the cabinet without a portfolio to oversee the functioning of the cabinet secretariat. Subsequently, Shastri and Indira Gandhi altered the powers and functioning of the PMS/PMO, while Rajiv Gandhi and Manmohan Singh brought in parliamentary secretaries and the MoS, respectively.

The PMO behaved better while working with non-Congress governments, as its interference in the functioning of the ministries was less due to coalition governments curtailing its administrative interference. Yet, if the PS commanded respect among his peers, the government's work could be expedited through better coordination between the PMO and the ministries. If the PS was known to have worked as the secretary in the ministries of home, defence, finance and external affairs located on Raisina Hill, he could command respect and be treated as being experienced in running the government. Since Haksar's days, principal secretaries have mostly been retired IAS and IFS officers who were senior to their serving officers in different ministries. Secretaries in the PMS, beginning with L.K. Jha who was upgraded to the cabinet secretary rank and allowed to attend cabinet meetings, were themselves relegated to the background after Haksar became the PS. Haksar, it may be clarified here, was appointed as the secretary in the PMS after L.K. Jha. Once he retired as secretary in 1971, he was again appointed as the PS; in his place was appointed P.N. Dhar, not an IAS or IFS, who played second fiddle to Haksar. So even after his retirement, Haksar kept on working in the PMS as the boss. And Dhar, despite serving as secretary, remained in a subordinate role.

This had a severe impact on the bureaucracy at large. The secretary, the serving officer who was the boss in the PMS during the Shastri years or perhaps even during the first term of Indira Gandhi, was relegated subsequently to the second, third and fourth positions. And the retired officers became his superiors. The chickens had come home to roost. The secretary and the PMS had usurped the power of the cabinet secretary during the Shastri years; now the PS had usurped the powers of the secretary. The appointment of the NSA and the principal advisors further pushed the secretary down the pecking order. Henceforth, retired civil servants were appointed as principal secretaries in the PMS-PMO by the prime ministers who, in practice, became the boss of the civil servants and more powerful than the cabinet secretary. Many cabinet secretaries—for example, Naresh Chandra—attempted to restore the warrant of precedence, but that was circumvented by the elevated rank of the principal secretaries who now had the rank of cabinet ministers. This kind of subversion of the roles and ranks of the cabinet secretariat and its secretary was seen widely during the Congress regimes. Non-Congress regimes continued with this subversion, as they failed to restore the old democratic and bureaucratic order of the collective functioning of the cabinet and its secretariat.

The Manmohan Singh regime brought about another innovation. The PM was not even willing to take credit for the positive work done by his government. Rather, the credit was being appropriated by the Gandhi family, who were projected as the messiah. However, their chosen PM was projected as a villain when the government faltered. The family had learnt their lesson from experiencing Narasimha Rao's tenure, who had run the government without any interference from them. This time the family intended to have their cake and eat it too. The idea was to seize the space of the Opposition by projecting Rahul Gandhi as the leader of the Opposition, should the citizens feel dissatisfied with the government. And credit was of course duly taken for any development work. The persona of the PM was also used for their benefit. He was just there on behalf of the family because Sonia Gandhi could not become the PM and Rahul Gandhi was not yet ready for the job, or rather he had miscalculated his ability.

The political standing of the PM was reflected in the PMO. He acted as the PS to Sonia Gandhi while running the administration. It was another novelty of the Congress regime where the party president was more powerful than the PM and the cabinet in running the government, as well as in selecting the members of the cabinet, the civil servants in the PMO, and for other offices. The Congress ministers were accountable to Sonia Gandhi. The leaders of the coalition parties and their ministers were more respectful to her. The PM was respected only for his integrity and knowledge. In comparison, Vajpayee was a towering figure despite a coalition government. His PS and NSA, Brajesh Mishra, was equally towering among his peers of civil servants. The restraint of coalition politics limited his powers as the PM; he could not select his cabinet ministers or enforce the party manifesto as the government policy; yet, due to his political standing, there was no match for Vajpayee in his cabinet or in the Opposition, which helped him in protecting his turf as PM. The PS successfully guarded him as well as derived his authority from Vajpayee's political-prime ministerial stature; Vajpayee, in turn, backed him to the hilt which was intended to protect his prime ministerial turf.

Coalition politics and the weak stature of the PM had one benefit: there was more democratic praxis in the cabinet functioning, and the interference of the PMO in the ministries was less. The PM became the first among equals, which resulted in the restoration of the cabinet secretariat as the prime agency of governmental coordination and monitoring. However, the effective and efficient application of decisions had slowed down even after the decisions in the cabinet were taken, as ministers belonging to different parties had their constituencies to cater to. That led to a substantive degree of autonomy in the functioning of the ministries, which many times were part of the prime ministerial turf, leading to ministerial fiefdoms with charges of corruption; this was starkly visible during Manmohan Singh's tenure, and the PM was helpless as he was not the boss. Many ministers ignored him and a few civil servants paid more attention to the party bosses. It was a classic case of accountability without political authority. Contrary to it, Brajesh Mishra, the PS and the NSA in the preceding Vajpayee government, had strengthened the authority of his PM despite running a coalition government. It was a classic case of the cabinet functioning effectively along with the PM equally enjoying his pre-eminence and authority.

Coalition governments may take longer to arrive at conclusions and make decisions in the cabinet, as different parties and their constituencies have different issues, lacking cohesive and compact programmes. Even on the issues of the Common Minimum Programme, the actual policy formulation may take longer due to the varied interpretations and requirements of different regions. Yet, there have been PMs and their PMOs who have handled the situation well during their tenures through regular monitoring of the ministries assigned for specific works.

Many times, the running of the office of the PM and its administration are substantively impacted by the personal traits of the occupants of the chair. In coalition politics in particular, asserting one's domain while co-opting divergent views may be better for running the government. In the case of Manmohan Singh, Sanjay Baru felt that he was less assertive, even on his turf, despite having the responsibility of running the government.[55] 'His unwillingness to confront and discipline his detractors in the party encouraged many of them to run with the hare and hunt with the hounds.'[56] This was also visible in the appointment of civil servants in the PMO and the ministries. Some of them quarrelled among themselves in front of the PM. It was an all-round decline in discipline, collective functioning and governance. Contrary to it, the succeeding Modi government, despite being a majority-party government, runs a coalition government and has successfully ironed out the differences that plagued the Manmohan Singh government.

The decline in the cabinet's functioning had become visible during Nehru's time itself, especially after the death of Patel in December 1950, when he let his ministers bypass the procedures of the cabinet with his consent. That facilitated his predominance over the cabinet instead of being the *primus inter pares*. His tendency to seek pre-eminence and limelight to gain popularity, domineer and interfere laid the foundations for running a prime ministerial government. He wanted to run the government according to his wishes, unlike the procedures and ethos of the cabinet which is collective, consensual, and where decisions are taken by the majority. The PM has to abide by the collective decisions, which is how the British cabinet has largely functioned over the years. Here, Nehru wanted the cabinet to function according to his own ideas or the ideas that he liked. He was open to contrarian views only under pressure, or when he felt helpless and there was no alternative left. Patel was highly critical of his approach in handling the cabinet and his methods of functioning. Nehru functioned through the cabinet secretariat; his PMS was small during the initial years and primarily coordinated the files.

The first time the PMS gained importance by serving in an advisory role was during Shastri's time, who laid the foundation of altering the pre-eminence of the cabinet secretariat by empowering his PMS with an advisory role and giving it a formal status equal to the cabinet secretariat.

Indira Gandhi altered it even further. She gave the PMS pre-eminence over the cabinet secretariat in practice, changing the rules by entrusting it to do political work, appointing retired officers in it, and interfering in the functioning of the ministries, thereby making the cabinet secondary; the cabinet functioned to satisfy the constitutional requirements for procedural and legal purposes. The Emergency was a classic case when the cabinet was not aware of its imposition; the appointment of Haksar as the PS after his retirement set another precedent that continues to date. Earlier, Shastri had introduced a couple of new precedents; the secretary in the PMS was elevated to the rank of the cabinet secretary. Prior to this, Nehru had initiated a new tradition of bringing his PPS to the cabinet meetings, in an attempt to imitate the viceroy. In 1947, after objections from cabinet colleagues, it was stopped. But after the death of Patel, he gradually started this practice again.

Even the rank and nomenclature of the secretary in the PMS was changed. Earlier, it was the PPS who was of joint secretary rank, which was subsequently changed. During Shastri's tenure, it was redesignated as secretary, who was elevated to the rank of cabinet secretary. Indira Gandhi had let Haksar rejoin as PS after his retirement; he was secretary while he was in service. It was unprecedented then for a retired officer to rejoin the PMS as the PS with a new designation, who effectively superseded the then secretary, P.N. Dhar. Earlier, Haksar was the secretary in the PMS, a rank and designation created by Shastri for L.K. Jha; Indira Gandhi inherited and adopted it; the rank was then superseded by Haksar as the PS, downgrading the rank of the secretary. Rajiv Gandhi added a new feature to it by appointing parliamentary secretaries in the PMO and expanded its staff further. Charan Singh had abolished the post of the PS, which was later restored by Indira Gandhi once she returned to power in January 1980.

The non-Congress governments adopted many of these 'innovations' of the Congress regimes. The Janata Party government, the first non-Congress government at the Centre, as well as the subsequent governments, such as the National Front (NF) and the National Democratic Alliance (NDA), adopted many features of the Congress regimes in the PMO. One, for example, was the appointment of principal secretaries in the PMO who were retired civil servants. When PM Desai appointed Vidya Shankar, there was a lot of hue and cry. It was taken so seriously post the Emergency that the President had to caution the PM. But Desai remained adamant and it subsequently became the new normal. However, many of the 'innovations' of the Congress regimes were not adopted due to the compulsions of coalition politics that the non-Congress governments found themselves in. It was only after the 1984 general elections that a non-Congress single-party government was formed in 2014 and in 2019, with a majority in the Lok Sabha.

The Non-Congress Years

In 1977, for the first time, a non-Congress government was formed under the prime ministership of Morarji Desai. For thirty years since Independence, the Congress had run the federal government under three different prime ministers, with their PMS gradually becoming a 'super cabinet', performing political, administrative, diplomatic and secretarial roles. It was Shastri who changed the mandate of his PMS, which was further expanded by Indira Gandhi. Under administrative heads like L.K. Jha and P.N. Haksar, the secretaries to the PMS, the PMS acquired larger tasks than the officially assigned work, which led to a rise in opposition to its political-administrative function for its interference in the other organs of administration and politics.

Morarji Desai

Once Desai took over as PM, he appointed Vidya Shankar as PS in the PMS, changed its name to PMO, and reduced its staff and profile. Viewed during the Emergency as an evil apparatus and with the hostility that had developed against it, its policy unit was dismantled. The interference of the PMO became less; the 'autonomy of departments and [the] powers of individual ministers' were respected. Decisions in the cabinet were unanimous and free. If the PM proposed a policy and the majority did not agree, the proposal was withdrawn.

This was in great contrast to the earlier situation when decisions were taken by the PM. Nehru, Shastri and Indira Gandhi used to summarize the cabinet meetings with their own decisions. Many times, particularly during the Nehru and Indira Gandhi years, procedures were not followed. Ministers, in consultation with the PMs, flouted cabinet procedures, and decisions taken by ministers in consultation with the PM were just reported in the cabinet meetings. Instead of an open discussion in the cabinet and collectively deciding, as decisions used to be taken before, decision-making became a pre-determined act. The Shastri tenure was more open, as the ministers used to speak their minds. The Indira years were the worst.

In comparison, Desai's tenure was open to ideas in cabinet meetings. The PMO did interfere but it was more in the affairs of the ministries and departments which were non-performing. Desai enforced prior cabinet clearance, particularly in terms of fiscal-financial issues, which was unlike the tenures of Nehru and Indira Gandhi. Both father and daughter had no patience to understand the nitty-gritties of fiscal-financial issues. They were more comfortable with the briefs prepared by their cabinet secretaries or the principal secretaries. Even Shastri was more dependent on his secretary L.K. Jha's notes. In contrast, Sardar Patel and Desai were willing to understand the fiscal details and would sit down with the ministers, experts and civil servants, listening to them and sorting out problems, if any.

Vidya Shankar's appointment was opposed by Desai's colleagues as he had retired and had also worked for corporate houses; it was considered unethical in the post-Emergency years to appoint such a person, who would, by nature, be privy to confidential papers. Desai argued that he knew his PS and trusted him; Shankar had worked with Sardar Patel since 1946. And it was more or less his discretion to appoint a person to the post. Shankar had experience in administration and public affairs and had the 'approach and qualification that would make Desai's task easy'.

It is interesting to read Desai's writings on the functioning of the cabinet. He considered his cabinet members as 'equals' and wanted the members to show 'respect for the joint responsibility'. Cabinet ministers trying to run their ministries as their own fiefdoms were rebuked; moreover, their different promises to different constituencies without the 'prior clearance of the cabinet' were not honoured. For instance, George Fernandes, Brijlal Verma and Chaudhary Charan Singh had made promises to their constituencies without the prior approval of the cabinet. Hence, Desai turned down their proposals for funds and policy application.

The critics of the Janata government, however, have argued that the concept of joint responsibility and prior clearance of the cabinet was selective, as it did not apply to Desai himself. For example, no prior cabinet clearance was taken to 'abjure (nuclear) explosions even for peaceful purposes'. In fact, it was never brought up to the cabinet; Desai had just announced it unilaterally.

The cabinet itself, it should be explained here, was not cohesive. It consisted of different political parties, primarily four, which were independent entities prior to their merger and emergence as the Janata Party. It was essentially a coalition of parties that had fused into one to oppose the regime of the Nehru dynasty, fuelled by the Emergency. Many of them were in the Opposition for years, so their habits continued despite becoming ministers. One-upmanship, inflated egos, and a lack of discipline destroyed the first non-Congress government in which the majority of them, except for the Jan Sangh members, were ex-Congressmen marginalized by Nehru, Shastri and Indira Gandhi. Morarji himself was a victim of his predecessors; the three prime ministers had politically marginalized him on different pretexts. Nehru had done it through the Kamaraj Plan, while the other two did not make him either the deputy PM or the number two in the cabinet; neither was he given important portfolios. He was eligible for the PM post after the death of Nehru, but to deny a strong personality like him the post, Shastri was made the PM by the Congress syndicate.

The Janata government did not complete its five-year tenure, but it restored the functioning of the cabinet and the cabinet secretariat and limited the role of the PMO. Advani, when interviewed by Limaye, stated that the general atmosphere in the Janata cabinet meetings used to be quite relaxed. For example, the PM had strong views on prohibition but he never tried to impose his views on the cabinet; they had the freedom to air their views unrestrained by the items on the agenda of the departments. The PMO, at the behest of the PM, never intervened in the affairs of the ministries. Even if the officers of the PMO did intervene, the PM may not have been aware of it. The files from Advani's ministry were never sent to the PMO. In cabinet meetings, decisions were recorded by the cabinet secretary[1] unlike during the time of Nehru or Shastri, who used to sum up and announce their decisions. During Indira Gandhi's tenure, after 1969, even this process withered away.

The most democratic functioning of the cabinet and its secretariat, Limaye felt, was between 1964 and 1969 and again between 1977 and 1979. These were periods when the prime ministers were not secure; there were internal political wrangling against them. The PMS-PMO therefore interfered less in the functioning of the ministries, particularly when the ministers were political heavyweights. Many times, the PMS-PMO interfered independently without the knowledge of the PM, as indicated by Advani in his interview.

Till 1950, or even later, the PPS to PM Nehru did not attend the cabinet meeting as part of the protocol. Only the cabinet secretary or the secretaries of the ministries used to be present when required. Nehru took his PPS Aiyangar to the cabinet meeting once when Patel was alive. There was resistance from the members of the cabinet and the civil servants, as it was not part of the cabinet convention. Nehru had to stop his initiative. He started it again after 1960. Shastri changed the mandate of the PMS officially in 1964, and his secretary in the PMS began to attend cabinet meetings. Subsequently, it became a normal routine. He also initiated a new step: his secretary began to formulate policies of the government on behalf of the cabinet, including the foreign policy. It no longer remained the exclusive domain of the cabinet and the cabinet secretariat. The PMS had begun to play the role of an equal partner, at par with the cabinet secretaries, if not the dominant partner, in running the administration. Nehru's PMS was kept away from such acts. Post Shastri, Indira Gandhi's PMS moved a step further in becoming the dominant partner. The cabinet secretariat was relegated to the background in the running of the government. Haksar, in fact, chaired the informal/non-cabinet diplomatic meetings and played an important role in the political affairs of the Congress, especially in the selection of the cabinet ministers. Nothing of the sort happened during the Morarji tenure.

Chaudhary Charan Singh

Chaudhary Charan Singh's tenure was insignificant; it was short and did not leave any imprint. The only significant part of his PMS was that he abolished the post of the PS, which had been created by Indira Gandhi for Haksar after his retirement in 1971; he was secretary to the PM. Subsequently, he was appointed as the PS for two years, till January 1973. So the changing nomenclature was as follows: the PPS to Nehru, the secretary to Shastri, the secretary and PS to Indira Gandhi, and then the secretary to Charan Singh. They were officers of the rank of joint secretary, secretary and cabinet secretary, mostly serving for a second term, except for retired civil servants Vidya Shankar and Haksar. Earlier, the PPS to Nehru in the 1950s were serving joint secretary-rank officers.

Charan Singh wanted to appoint G.V.K. Rao as his PS, who had retired. Rao refused and suggested that he appoint a serving officer. Charan Singh then appointed Krishna Rao Sahib and abolished the post of the PS. The appointment of Vidya Shankar, a retired officer, had created a controversy during Morarji's time. President Reddy wrote a letter to the PM against creating such a convention. Once Indira Gandhi came back to power in January 1980, P.C. Alexander was appointed as the PS. Rao Sahib continued in his post for five months after Indira Gandhi's return to power in her second term.

The PMO once again returned to its worst self. Indira Gandhi began a new convention by starting to meet the secretaries of different ministries; the files began to be routed through the PMO. It was the culmination of the downfall of the cabinet system. Even the apparent semblance of a cabinet-led government was done away with. It was the prime ministerial government which was operational at that point. The Janata party government had put the cabinet government back on the rails, but the convention was once again reversed.

V.P. Singh to I.K. Gujral

The V.P. Singh, Chandra Shekhar, and National Front governments of Deve Gowda and I.K. Gujral were again short-term governments. These governments were formed out of a coalition of multiple parties, including parties not in government but providing outside support; the largest parties were not in the government.

Coalition Era: 1989–2014

In fact, for 25 years, from 1989 to 2014 (when Narendra Modi formed the government), it was the era of coalition politics as the electorate did not vote any single party into power, resulting in the lack of majority votes for any one party in the Lok Sabha. In other words, it took 25 years for the Indian electorate to vote for a single-party majority (BJP) government. The Congress government headed by Narasimha Rao had achieved a majority through defection. The fragmented non-Congress Opposition had failed to unite against the Congress. Even the Janata party, formed in 1977 out of a merger of four different parties, failed to remain united.

The socio-political aspirations of different castes, fragmentarily reflected in the different political parties—particularly in asymmetrical regional variations—needed a powerful centripetal organization with a leadership to hold them together. This was sorely lacking. The non-Congress, non-BJP coalitions delegated more and were more democratic, but they lacked cohesive, binding organization. The PMO, therefore, was more reticent and subtle, for the existence of its bosses was uncertain. The Congress-led coalition governments, on the other hand, were more certain of their tenures despite being in coalition or managing governments without a majority in the Lok Sabha; this holds for both the Narasimha Rao and Manmohan Singh governments.

There were two binding forces for coalition governments. First, the Nehru dynasty glued the rootless Congress leaders to the party; the mostly regional non-BJP opposition parties, full of ex-Congressmen, were equally dynastic. The second factor was the corruption—political, business and administrative—that oiled the parties, glued them, and actuated the anarchic functioning of the administrative machinery under the rubric of development. The message of the electorate against the Congress system, reflected in the electoral verdict in the Lok Sabha represented by the fragmented party system, was thus lost. While the Congress used the fragmentary verdict successfully, the non-Congress parties failed three times to complete their tenures—first during 1977–79, second during 1989–91, and third during 1996–98. It was only from 1998 onwards that the BJP could emerge as a powerful political alternative to the Congress, and as the cohesive force that could glue the other parties to provide an alternative government. Once in a position to last a full term, the PMO regained its 'power' to an extent during Vajpayee's tenure.

The V.P. Singh, Chandra Shekhar, Charan Singh, Deve Gowda and I.K. Gujral governments restored the functioning of the cabinet, following what Desai had done during 1977–79; the ministries became autonomous in their functioning and the interference of the PMO stopped. The PMO did assist the PM in the decision-making process, but it was not the policymaking body. Many of the posts within it were abolished, for the ministries now enjoyed autonomy. As a result, the functioning of the PMO was streamlined and its powers were restricted. The Foreign Investment Promotion Board, which was created by Narasimha Rao under the liberalization process for 'single-window clearance', however, remained within the PMO. Rao was not happy with the sluggish functioning of his PMO and wrote notes to the British PM to understand the functioning of the British PMS.

B.G. Deshmukh, the PS, felt that the PMO was a necessity, and he was not alone. Most civil servants who worked in the PMO felt similarly. But others who did not work there did not necessarily think in the same way. In terms of power relations, the PMO enjoyed an upper hand; therefore, for those who worked there, the PMO was a necessity; subsequently, many justificatory arguments followed. Nehru functioned with only secretarial assistance. The British cabinet runs the administration with its cabinet secretariat, and the PMS only provides secretarial assistance to the PM. Margaret Thatcher and Tony Blair, however, changed the structure and the mandate of their PMS, which now continues to function substantively in its pre-Thatcher form. Prime ministers following Blair discontinued the roles and powers appropriated by the PMS, which were part of the roles of the cabinet secretary.

Atal Bihari Vajpayee

The formation of the BJP-led government in 1998 once again led to a partial acquisition of power by the PMO, despite it being in a coalition government. PM Vajpayee appointed Brajesh Mishra as the NSA with the rank of minister of state and also as the PS.

The creation of the post of the NSA was a new innovation, with its own council and secretariat. This creation and combination of posts brought about unprecedented power to the PMO, even in a coalition government, against the backdrop of the political standing of Vajpayee, who had contested the election as the prime ministerial candidate of the BJP-led coalition.

But Vajpayee's 'administrative style was not centralized'; it 'involved appropriate delegation'. He had 'efficient managerial abilities'[2], yet he was 'the ultimate boss without seeming like one'.[3] His cabinet functioned on consensus and the ministers expressed their views freely. Vajpayee listened to them and then moved on to build consensus through summarizing the views in his own inimical style.[4] The ideas and suggestions were incorporated into the pre-programmed agenda. Divergent views and political conflicts were ironed out at the parties' meetings through the Common Minimum Programme. The political executive, comprising diverse political views, accepted Vajpayee as their leader for he had the largest support of the electorate. Also, the BJP itself had dropped the contentious programme from its manifesto that facilitated its gelling together with others. The nuclear explosion created a sense of pride that reinforced his political authority. Alongside this, the re-emergence of the BJP as the single-largest party third time in a row catapulted his stature.

Once stability was entrenched, the PMO became active. But it was not the re-enactment of the Indira Gandhi/Rajiv Gandhi years, as the Vajpayee government was a coalition government made up of diverse parties. The officers in the PMO were sensitive enough to understand these nuances; Vajpayee himself was enough of a realist to restrain his officers from jumping the gun. In fact, the officers in the PMO behave according to the stature and gestures of their prime ministers.[5] If the government is stable and the authority of the PM permeates, the PMO begins to intervene in the administration. Many times, however, the PMs are unaware of the nitty-gritties of the actions of their officers in the PMO. It violates or, out of exuberance, breaks the hierarchy of the officialdom. For example, the agenda, programmes of the day, etc., in the case of Vajpayee were decided by Brajesh Mishra and others in the PMO. N.M. Ghatate, R.V. Pandit and Sudheendra Kulkarni were some of the others who worked with Vajpayee.

What was new in the Vajpayee regime was the creation of the post of NSA which was bestowed upon Brajesh Mishra, who was also the PS and was given the rank of MoS. Advani would later observe that Mishra should not have been given two posts as it affected governance.[6] Many times, he was sent abroad as the personal envoy of the PM without prior consultation with the foreign minister. Similarly, many of the files of the ministry of defence, without the clearance of the NSA, were sent to the PM. Derivatively, it reflects that even in coalition governments, principal secretaries command an important role depending on the stature of the PM.

In the appointment of Brajesh Mishra, Vajpayee's very first appointment order issued for him, their broad agreements over the Nuclear Test Ban Treaty, the Chemical Weapons Conventions, the 'intention to exercise the nuclear option', and a broader thrust on foreign policy played an important role. Mishra was the convener of the BJP cell on foreign policy, assisting the party in writing its manifesto. In Vajpayee's first term, the PS was Bishan Tandon, who was also the joint secretary during Indira Gandhi's tenure in the 1970s. Tandon was expecting reappointment but that did not fructify. Mishra, over the next six years, acquired the image of a larger-than-life persona of the 'Bharat Sarkar', as Gopal Krishna Gandhi would write in his obituary.[7]

Over the past two decades, since Vajpayee approved the formation of the National Security Board and appointed the advisor, there has been an intermittent shift in the making of foreign policy. It became linked with the inputs of the security establishment, particularly when pertaining to relations with immediate neighbours. The policy of terror as an instrument of state in relation to the neighbouring nations promoted the shift; the nuclear explosion only expedited the process. This resulted in the appropriation of more powers by the NSA and the PMO, best demonstrated at the time when the bomb was exploded in the Thar Desert.

The NSA or the PS also acted as special envoy, if required, for the prime ministers to portray an image of commanding political clout. It was also to bypass the normal officialese to enable the PM to informally exchange views with the other side and arrive at a solution or at least narrow down differences. Such measures were also initiated in the past; the only difference now was that there was a new post of the NSA, with a new mandate.

When the bomb explosion was taking place in the Thar Desert, it was being monitored at the PM's residence-cum-office at 7, Race Course Road (RCR), by a team of officials led by Brajesh Mishra, Prabhat Kumar (cabinet secretary), K. Raghunath (foreign secretary) and Shakti Sinha (Vajpayee's PS). Vajpayee had also appointed Pramod Mahajan as his political adviser with the rank of a cabinet minister. Such acts of the non-Congress prime ministers were partly a legacy of the past and partly a new requirement emerging out of new situations with concerns about security and strategy. But it also overshadowed the roles and domains of other ministries. Many times, the ministries resented; other times, they overlooked the interventions. Brajesh Mishra and Haksar were more indulgent. As they were from the foreign service, they also intervened in the making of foreign policy. Rasgotra, the foreign secretary during Indira Gandhi's tenure, once told me that in his ministry, he had his emphatic say in making foreign policy.

Despite heading a coalition government, Vajpayee's six-year tenure remained largely centred on him; the selection of ministers, their numbers and portfolios were compromised. It was not his sole discretion to select them, but his dominance as the PM was far greater in comparison to other prime ministers of other coalition governments. Challenges came but were brushed aside, as Rao had done earlier. It was unlike the tenure of Gujral or Morarji Desai, who were politically challenged or would be shouted down in meetings. Cabinet colleagues who tried to browbeat Rao during cabinet meetings were removed. The PMOs of both Rao and Vajpayee—one being a coalition government and the other a minority government—functioned accordingly, as per the stature of their respective bosses.

Ministers who had had a long political standing with a wide electoral-social base, or those who were of different political parties with substantive numbers of parliamentarians, ran their ministries with a long rope. Vajpayee, however, was not defied despite the absence of BJP's majority at the Centre or in many states; his presence was acknowledged. But the intervention of his PMO was not entertained in the routine functioning of the ministries headed by the ministers of non-BJP parties in the coalition. AIADMK's Thambi Durai, the minister of corporate affairs, for example, was under strict instructions from his party's boss to stonewall any proposal that came from the PMO to initiate change in governance. Jayalalitha and Mamata Banerjee tried to defy Vajpayee in their own ways, but they did not succeed. The electorate voted for Vajpayee. He came back to power again in 1999 after the withdrawal of support by Jayalalitha. He returned to power in 1998 despite the refusal of the political parties to form a government under his leadership. Officials in the PMO often sent routine queries to different ministries, of which the PM would be unaware. Earlier, Desai's PMO was not entertained by many ministers who were from different ideological or political backgrounds. The PM had to make compromises to run the government. In the case of Vajpayee and Desai, there were serious objections even in the appointments of their principal secretaries. Shankar's appointment by Desai and Mishra's appointment by Vajpayee—their principal secretaries, respectively—were opposed by different people for administrative, political and ethical reasons. In Shankar's case, it was an administrative and ethical issue, for he had retired and was working with private corporate houses; in Mishra's case, it was a political and administrative point, as he wielded too much power—he represented PM Vajpayee as a special envoy to different countries and led the official team constituting the cabinet and foreign secretaries; procedurally, the protocol was adhered to, but in effect it subverted the role of the cabinet and its secretariat.

In the name of teamwork, speed, secrecy, efficiency and delivery, the cabinet government was transformed into a prime ministerial government. The power of the PMO or the status of the PS reflected the nature of the government, whether it was prime ministerial or cabinet in form. Even in the coalition governments, the position of the PMO did not revert to the era of 1947–50. In the post-Patel era, there was a gradual move towards the prime ministerial form; and from 1972, only the procedural part of the cabinet largely remained in one-party dominant governments. The soul of the collective functioning represented by the cabinet incrementally withered away. Only the coalition governments could restrain the prime ministerial form.

The formation of different committees of the cabinet, first introduced in Britain during World War II, aided by different officials, experts and modern technologies, facilitated the move towards the prime ministerial form. It has been an evolutionary trajectory combined with the intent of prime ministers to move towards the American presidential form without altering the form of the cabinet system. Some prominent British ex-colonies like Canada, Australia and India have adopted this method. Britain itself has been very slow in this direction, despite numerous attempts by different prime ministers, which still makes it a substantively cabinet government.

Modern technologies have made administration transparent, efficient and connected, facilitating governance. It has created new opportunities and space for citizens and the administration. It keeps the PM connected to his office no matter where he goes, so he can take decisions and consult his ministers, officials and experts. This has, in turn, facilitated the speed of collective governance. Earlier, the absence of modern technologies would force the PM to be physically present for a collective decision. The fear of political instability also forced prime ministers to follow collective governance.

In Vajpayee's cabinet meetings, there were free discussions; the final decisions, however, were summed up by him. 'He trusted specialists to do their job,' insulating economic growth from the politics of the day. It resulted in the formation of the

PM's economic advisory council, a new body. It was felt that this move would undermine the finance ministry, which had its own economic advisers. Many such moves were criticized. Dattopant Thengadi (the founder of Bharatiya Mazdoor Sangh, Swadeshi Jagran Manch, and Bharatiya Kisan Sangh) charged Vajpayee as being a 'petty politician playing into the hand of his policy advisors with doubtful credentials.'[8] The Swadeshi Jagran Manch also felt Vajpayee's top advisers were 'from the past regimes and had their agenda'. Mishra was inevitably part of every meeting as the PS or as the NSA. He was the son of a Congress chief minister. Vajpayee was open to criticisms of his ideas, as he felt the critics' perceptions may vary; he did not accept every critic as a political opponent or antagonist, as his focus was on good governance.

The PMO grew in stature, as the officials working with the PM commanded his trust. It may not necessarily have been the case for every official, but senior officers working in the proximity of the PM were expected to command the trust of their boss. Mathai in the case of Nehru, Haksar or Dhawan in the case of Indira Gandhi, Pulok Chatterjee and Vincent George in the case of Rajiv Gandhi and Sonia Gandhi, Brajesh Mishra in the case of Vajpayee, or P.K. Mishra in the case of Modi are a few relevant examples. The trust may be due to the familiarity of working together or recommendations by trusted persons. Since the Shastri years, many of the decisions and appointments—political and administrative—by the PM have been taken in consultation with or on the advice of such officials.

In single-party governments, prime ministers enjoy larger autonomy in decision-making. In coalition governments, such autonomy is limited. Yet Vajpayee enjoyed substantive autonomy in appointments and decision-making in the administration, in the coordination committee of the coalition parties, and in the government. He created space for his manoeuvrability through deft handling of the parties, creating new offices and appointing experts in the field. While in government, he was charged for perpetuating a communal agenda by his political opponents; after his death, he is fondly remembered for being secular and democratic.

Narendra Modi

Modi's PMO is the most digitalized, responsive and transparent office in comparison to those of his predecessors. As the PM, he has expedited and expanded the use of technology for governance to the hilt in terms of actuating transparency, accountability, effectiveness and responsiveness in the functioning of ministries and the administration. It has resulted in the delivery of quality services to citizens and acted as a deterrent to the corrupt.

He began with two immediate measures after he took over as the PM in 2014. He brought in an ordinance to remove legal obstacles to appoint Nripendra Mishra as his PS. Second, he brought the appointment of OSDs to ministers under the Appointments Committee of the Cabinet (ACC). Earlier, OSDs were not under the purview of the ACC; ministers used to bring in their confidants as OSD. Prior to this, Mishra, as the chairperson of the Telecom Regulatory Authority of India (TRAI), was ineligible for appointment. These two acts of Modi reflected the intent of the PM to be decisive, and to cleanse the polity in the preceding political backdrop of the role of the NAC chaired by Sonia Gandhi and of the PMO of Manmohan Singh. This was followed by meetings with secretaries of different ministries and permitting them access to the PM to expedite the formulation and application of developmental schemes, side-stepping procedural hurdles. Earlier, Indira Gandhi had initiated this process in 1980, which was then considered to be breaking the protocol of collective governance.

Another novelty in the PMO was the creation of the post of additional PS; P.K. Mishra, who was appointed to the post, was to assume the charge of the PS during Modi's second term in 2019, with a new elevation to the cabinet rank. In fact, all three—the PS, the additional PS and the NSA—were elevated to this rank. Later on, Nripendra Mishra resigned, and hence their responsibilities and work distribution, including that of the NSA, were divided. While the NSA looks after 'policies and matters (except appointments) relating to Ministries of External affairs, Overseas Indian Affairs, Defence, Space, Atomic Energy, NSCN and R&AW/RAS,' the PS looks after the 'policy issues and matters relating to Ministries of Personnel, Public Grievances & Pensions and Law & Justice, Appointments Committee of the Cabinet and other appointments, Cabinet Secretariat, listing of Cabinet items, Anti-corruption Unit, PMO Establishment; all important policy issues and matters'[9] (Annexure I). The division of work eliminated the confusion that had plagued Manmohan Singh's PMO. In fact, the very genesis of the emergence of the PMO, as L.K. Jha explained long back, was to prevent 'the inefficient way of conducting Government business'.

During the Nehru years, as Jha continues, 'whenever a proposal was put to him...he would answer promptly, yes, I agree or no, I have doubts, and he would pass the matter on to the appropriate Ministry for detailed consideration; later, when this issue came before cabinet he would put his mind to it; and, not infrequently, at the late stage [he] would reject the proposal, with the result that the effort in preparing material would be wasted.' To prevent it, an administrative arm (PMS) like any other ministry was created during the Shastri years to keep the PM informed and advise him whenever required. This subsequently became a permanent arm but, as explained earlier, remained an office only to efficiently provide advice and information to the PM. It had no authority, *de jure locus standi*, like the department of a ministry. The office was just a replica of the department. It had no power to direct, command or punish any officer in the ministry or in any autonomous organization under the ministry. The ministry as a unit of governance remained supreme. Over it was the cabinet, which could intervene, and above all was the parliament. As the PM coordinated the works of his cabinet, the PS began to coordinate the secretarial works of different ministries, leading to 'the decline of the Cabinet Secretary to the role of clearing house for cabinet papers'. And as retired civil servants began to be appointed to the PS post, who were earlier senior in service compared to the serving cabinet secretary, with ever-elevating ranks in the protocol, the importance of the cabinet secretary further declined, and more so when access to the PM began to be regulated by the PMO.

It has been argued that with the rise of the PM as the chief executive and the pre-eminent political actor, there have emerged advisors and assistants to aid their bosses, enabling them to serve their responsibilities and duties towards the political society which elects them. It may look like the presidentialization of the powers of the PM in the cabinet form of government; but in the case of coalition governments, this does not work. The problem begins when these aides, advisors and assistants begin to intervene, without a mandate, in different spheres of administration and politics instead of remaining confined to their domain. The influence, patronage and command over resources have strengthened the undesirable growth of the unelected executive over the legislature, which often leads to their tyranny over the other without any public accountability. This also leads to the PM's image being maligned; in the politics of the contest for leadership, perception among the electorate plays an important role. It may be stated here that from the second half of the twentieth century, policy initiatives and decision-making have pre-eminently become the domain of the PM in a one-party government, or through the instrumentality of the PMO, which attempt to rein in coalition partners in case of a coalition government. This has led to the 'superseding' of the collective decision-making process, which has in turn encouraged the critique of the prime ministerial form.

Modi has been careful in perception management. He does not bank on his officers for political roles. The public visibility of the officers in the PMO has been low; their powers are defined. The political decisions are taken by Modi himself, unlike Shastri who was substantively dependent on L.K. Jha, while Indira Gandhi banked on Haksar. Modi has, of course, elevated the rank of his officers and created new posts—for example, the additional PS (in his first term) or the principal advisor (in his second term)—but their roles are strictly defined. The principal adviser, P.K. Sinha, looks after the 'policy issues and matters relating to all ministries/ Departments/agencies/bodies except those specifically allocated to Principal Secretary to PM and NSA.'[10] The post of the additional PS held by P.K. Mishra was abolished in the second term once Nripendra Mishra resigned in August 2020 from his post and

P.K. Mishra was elevated to his post. As the additional PS, P.K. Mishra was assigned the duty of looking after the appointments committee of the cabinet. P.K. Sinha, the principal advisor, also resigned in March 2021, followed by the resignation of Amarjeet Sinha, the special advisor, in August 2021.

Modi and other prime ministers have been flexible in the appointment of aides and support staff in the PMO with different designations and roles, as per their capabilities and the requirements of the PMs. One aspect, however, is noticeable: while many prime ministers have media advisors who interact with the press, clarify doubts, explain the government's or the PM's positions, Modi has no such advisor. His officers, on the other hand, analyze media content and report it to Modi. Accordingly, different mediums are used to convey messages on behalf of the PM. The more effective and widely disseminated the messages are, the better it is for the PM and the government; fortunately, Modi's methods have been very effective so far. Being technology-savvy and sensitive to social-cultural-political developments, the officers use various technologies and mediums to create a mesmerizing impact on the citizens. They also produce a spectacle through the scale, size and volume of the imprints on the perception of the citizens, creating an image of the PM as a messiah. This image and the appropriate words chosen for it, along with his works and communication skills in the public domain, have made him invincible in the political and public spheres.

The kind of persons he chooses, whether Jagdish Thakkar or Hiren Joshi, who remain invisible and work with precision and timing, makes Modi a master strategist. These officers keep an eye over different mediums across the country and the world, and react accordingly. More importantly, they initiate new imagery and thought processes among the citizens to keep their boss one step ahead of his political competitors; for this, different languages and agencies are used. This method of communication is one unique aspect of Modi in handling the media that separates him from the others. He does not carry the press along with himself, the way past prime ministers used to; rather, his power to create the spectacle mesmerizes the media which follows him and, in turn, becomes the instrument of generating the mass spectacle. Radio, apps, emails and digital platforms are used innovatively to directly interact with the masses instead of being dependent on journalists and their mediums to disseminate the messages of the PM and the government. The other prime ministers were dependent on journalists. In the case of Modi, journalists are dependent on him. He uses new technology and mediums to break and create news.

Many of the rules, which had become anachronisms, have been either deleted or changed. Many of the rules that had not been applied have been innovatively applied. The changes have come while learning from the inadequacies detected in the process of application. Many times, it was felt that the direct monitoring by the PMO may expedite the developmental process. A case in point is the project monitoring group, which was created as a cell within the cabinet secretariat in 2013 to monitor the status of projects. In 2014, it was brought within the ambit of the PMO.

The appointments of the OSDs and the PS of ministers were brought under the purview of the ACC. Many of the powers of the cabinet ministers, however, were gradually brought under the purview of the PM, long before Modi became the PM. A comparative study of the Allocation of Business Rules of the past 60 years will reflect the stated fact (Annexure II). Here, it is important to state that in 1961, as per the Allocation of Business Rule, the PMS was in Serial No. 24. In 2020, the PMS slid down to Serial No. 90, which reflects that in the pre-Modi years, a host of other domains were brought under the purview of the PM. What he has done anew is streamlining and digitalizing its functioning. From 1964, the files from the cabinet secretariat to the PMO and back have been doing the rounds. Usually, a file makes two rounds before it is approved by the cabinet. Modi has systematized, formalized and expedited the operational and procedural parts.

Within the cabinet, the traditional EGOMs and the Groups of Ministers have been transformed into I/E groups, which has reduced paperwork. The inputs of the National Security Council and other think tanks, governmental and non-governmental, are factored into the making of any policy, particularly related to economic issues, national security and foreign policy. It has widened the ambit from the traditional domains of the ministries and governmental organizations to the new domain of think tanks.

A part of the national security framework is the new set-up of the Defence Planning Committee, which is chaired by the NSA and constitutes the three service chiefs, the foreign secretary, the defence secretary, the expenditure secretary, and the chairperson of the Integrated Defence Staff, who acts as member secretary and also as the deputy Chief of the Defence Staff (CDS); the post of the CDS was created in 2019 during Modi's second term. The creation of the post had been under consideration since PM Vajpayee's years. Many of the pending decisions have thus been implemented, the most important being the modernization of the army as part of the national security framework, for which the related ministries are prodded to be prompt in innovating new methods. Economic development is of course the premise and the top priority over which the military edifice is created. It's more like Patel's three pillars to strengthen India: the agenda of governance, the rapid development of the economy, and the strengthening of the armed forces.

The number of staff in the PMO at present is approximately 300, far less than the staff during the tenure of Rajiv Gandhi or Vajpayee. The present annual budget is approximately INR 65 crore. It is not a department but comes under the Transactions/Allocation of Business Rules, 1961, which have been amended from time to time in the past 60 years. It is an extra-constitutional part of Article 77 of the Constitution, which deals with the PM and the council of ministers. In its functioning, it is different from other departments. The staff, from assistants to section officers, and from directors to the secretary, assist the PM with different tasks, including his speeches. It seeks factually correct information from different governmental and non-governmental agencies.

Most of the information regarding the PMO is available on the official digital platform or can be sought through the Right to Information (RTI) Act. Many of the contemporary file notes, however, are not shared. As the secretary to the PM in the PMS became his advisor, since 1964, the post has not remained confined to the role of the secretarial assistant. It was bestowed with the power to advise and initiate policy formulation; but the role of the PMS/PMO has since changed. Legally, the role still provides 'secretarial assistance', but in substance its role has been transformed; that's why the 'ghost file' and the file notes began and acquired the status of being confidential. The whole development since 1964 is thus the actualization of the idea of Nehru, who had sought a powerful secretariat (PMS) in 1947.

Shastri and Indira Gandhi made it functional, and this has been carried forward subsequently. In Canada, such a development is discussed as 'presidentializing' the powers of the PM.

The PMO has always been open to the recruitment of staff from different fields. But it was largely dominated by civil servants, particularly IFS and IAS officers of different ranks. The role of media advisors or public relation officers would usually be given to journalists or editors. During the Modi tenure, the office has seen wider openings for new expertise; the focus is on new ideas and new methods of their application. From electoral reform to the delimitation of constituencies and wards, from digitalizing the tendering process to bringing in new entrants in the administration—candidates from the non-IAS category as well as the corporate world are entering the ministries and departments in the ranks of higher administrative grades—the changes are visible.

The government offices, dominated by civil servants and power brokers, habituated to traditional methods of functioning, are now more transparent and open to public suggestions through the digital platform. It has led to two-way interactions: participation in governance and the participation of the administration in understanding public grievances and necessities. Many times, the public has suggested the best ways to solve the problems plaguing them. The linking of Aadhaar cards with bank accounts for the direct transfer of money in the accounts of designated beneficiaries under different governmental schemes, which has minimized the leakage of funds, is another marked innovative administrative reform. Digital platforms have also been used to develop a connect between citizens and the ministries, including their different wings, as the views and proposals of the public for social change are sought; if found feasible, the public's ideas have been transformed into government policy. This has minimized wasteful expenses and de-clogged delivery mechanisms.

The noticeable feature of the functioning of the PMO is to select honest and efficient civil servants from across the different tiers of services and hierarchies, who have innovative mechanisms of delivery, and place them in key positions; it is to weed out corrupt and inefficient civil servants, bring in new technology/tools for transparency, involve citizens in policymaking, and minimize the role of lobbyists and middle men in the functioning of the administration. To expedite delivery, Modi also directly interacts with the chief secretaries and district collectors of different states where projects have been pending for long. The idea is to create a level-playing field for different regions which have been lagging in infrastructural development. Chief ministers have been asked to share best practices of the executions of different schemes and projects in their states for universal application.

It may be interesting to learn that Modi used to consult Lee Kuan Yew of Singapore in administrative matters, and was inspired by the reformist Sayajirao Gaekwad of the erstwhile princely state of Baroda.[11] This has resulted in digital change and other innovations, forcing ministers and officers to be constantly at work, tracking the degree of development in each ministry and each state where central schemes and funds are involved. Such monitoring has led to the rapid execution of projects which have been languishing for years, resulting in the completion of projects on time. Ideas on digital platforms shared by citizens from across India are passed on to the different ministries to be analyzed. Once its feasibility is approved, with the collated data from the ministry, it is sent to the PMO for approval. Once approved, these ideas become policies for application. Different policies which are applicable today are either premised on the Gujarat experience or were formulated in the past ten years.

Uday Mahurkar, a journalist and political analyst, provides graphic details of the functioning of the team. It collects and collates the data on the digital platform of the MyGov app, and shares it with the PMO and the ministries. The point to be noted here is that there are dedicated volunteers across India who assist the government. They are 'researchers…analyzing the data as a service to the nation.'[12] More interesting is the fact that the PM himself suggested that the citizens on this app assess the functioning of his government in an online poll. And the number of citizens voting affirmatively for the policies online have been substantively large—larger than the numbers engaged by any single media house for any survey conducted by them at different times.

Such critical public appraisal has put him on a high moral pedestal that makes him unamenable to extraneous influences of caste, religion or region. He chooses his officers purely on the basis of merit, whether they are technology savvy, and possession of innovative ideas, integrity and efficiency. The way the bureaucracy was functioning for itself in the states—and in the preceding central governments through different kinds of lobbies—needed strong measures of correction and monitoring. Bringing in the OSDs and PS to the ministers under the purview of the ACC was one such early measure taken by Modi to check lobbying. His directive to his top officers in the PMO and the cabinet secretariat was to identify upright officers without any extraneous considerations. The traditional method of selecting an officer based on his Annual Confidential Report (ACR) was no longer valid, as 90 per cent of the officers had a very high grade of appraisal, which had become the norm after 2008. To overcome it, a new real-time rating was constructed based on due diligence, learnt from the method adopted by the New Zealand government. Also, learning from Indian corporates like the TATA Group and countries like the USA, the UK and others, four main criteria were fixed upon. One was the integrity and efficiency of the officers, verified by peer groups, batchmates, seniors and juniors. The other requirements would be functional skills, 'domain expertise' and 'behavioural competencies'. 'Once an officer is cleared through this process, his or her name enters the retention pool…next the name is sent to the Central Services Board (CSB) to match his job profile… Here the secretaries of the departments are also involved. Once the name is finalized, the CSB sends it to the ACC which clears it within 24 hours.'[13] The process is applicable to different services, which has resulted in the vertical and lateral mobility of many non-IAS officers to different posts. A similar kind of due diligence in appointments is being followed in other services such as banks, the public sector, and paramilitary/police organizations. Many of the top-ranking posts in such organizations, earlier occupied by IAS/IPS officers, are now occupied by in-house officers of the concerned organizations. It has generated a sense of belonging and commitment towards their organizations. Plus, it has also de-clogged opportunities for vertical mobility for in-house subordinate officers. The process, however, is yet to percolate deeply and widely. The coalition politics in Modi's third term may slow down the application.

Modi looks at officers and the administration as a facilitator, a delivery mechanism; the different ministries and departments and their wings need to coordinate for efficient functioning; for that, he conducts regular meetings with the heads of the administration, from the ministers and mayors of municipalities to the district magistrates (DMs) and secretaries. In this process, he has broken many protocols. The different ministries and departments, in the name of autonomy, were earlier not coordinating with each other, resulting in delays in their work or their coordination meetings being just paperwork. Actual delivery was lacking. Now it's the kind of teamwork that transcends ministerial/departmental boundaries, leading to a quantum change in the performance of the administration while strictly following official procedures. Many times, to make the process smooth, the government has laid down new procedures of selection, coordination and functioning. One may find it interesting to note that ministers in state governments, particularly of opposition parties, write to the PM to expedite the completion of stalled projects in their states.

The different ministries have been advised to share the development works of their ministries with the public on social media, which can be tracked using MyGov. Training sessions have been organized to explain the procedures to the ministries and their officials. Even their rating score was initiated on a weekly basis.[14] NITI Aayog plays an equally important role in policy inputs, drafting, recommending and advising the government. Structural and institutional reforms can be suggested to make administration transparent and efficient in delivery. They can also create new opportunities by opening up new vistas to focus on empowering citizens.

Cabinet meetings are not a procedural formality. For the agenda to be discussed in meetings, the concerned ministry's proposals are discussed in advance and in minute detail with the PMO. Suggestions, if any, about the feasibility of their application are incorporated in a proposal before it is put on the agenda. The ministry and the cabinet discuss it further with new inputs, if any. If the coordination of other ministries is required, they are also roped in. In fact, other ministries are roped in at the preliminary planning stage itself, before the agenda is brought to the cabinet. The floor is open to suggestions and discussions; it is constructive and productive. Any loophole or gap is discussed and rectified. Public suggestions are sought through digital and other platforms. Their feedback is used to fix issues, if any. The frequency and duration of Cabinet meetings, apart from the routine and the procedural, depend on the requirements, and so they may go on for hours.

Modi is a stickler for procedure. In the PMO, the different officers have their assigned roles. Taking benefit of their positions for personal gain or for the sake of joy is not tolerated. The office works as a cohesive, efficient functional unit. The officers are selected through a system of feedback on their performance in a preceding assignment. Young officers with their new ideas and innovative methods of applications are equally important; they are invited to work with the team. Talent from outside the cadre is equally given a chance to demonstrate their capabilities. Departmental/sectional dominance or maintaining exclusiveness, not coordinating or being reluctant to coordinate with others, or maintaining political-ministerial turf, are not acceptable actions.

The government is not a loose conglomerate of the ministries, the departments and the PMO, or a concoction of federalized units. Rather, it's an integrated, cohesive unit with substantive autonomy, one that is impeccably committed to working for the citizens while simultaneously ensuring the application of the rule of governance in deeds. Meticulous planning to the last detail, with alternatives in case of an emergency, is the hallmark of this government, which has been visible for the past ten years. Quick responses, with sensitive handling of situations in international and national domains, have been amply demonstrated multiple times. Unintentional errors emerging out of unpredictable situations are rectified. But casual, negligent acts leading to errors are swiftly punished. Modi is sensitive to the popular perception of his government; how the citizens look at his government and everyday administration is an important factor for him. His hard work and constant encouragement to officers selected on the basis of their performance are visible to all. He leads from the front by dint of example, not overlooking or ignoring any domain of administration which is either slow to act or non-performing or discriminatory in policy and deeds. If required, Modi addresses deputy collectors, deputy commissioners, DGPs, chief secretaries, mayors and panchayat heads, persuading them to work diligently in their assigned areas, asking them about administrative obstacles, seeking suggestions, and suggesting ways to overcome problems. What is visible in his functioning style is that he is a hard taskmaster and disciplinarian, working as per a programmatic schedule and expecting others to work accordingly as a team.

Following his nudge to chief secretaries and officers in the districts and states, a silent administrative reform was initiated at the district level, where the district collectors' traditional role was delegated and decentralized to circle officers. The district collectors are now the policy coordinators in the districts, following the pattern of chief secretaries in the states. Their primary tasks now are to facilitate GDP growth in their districts, enhance revenue collections, and look after governance and development.[15] This is because the district is now being developed as the primary unit of GDP measurement for comparative analyses to judge their performance in the country.

Some states, such as Assam, have already initiated the work. In the reform agenda, the district collectors' new work has been enlisted, and their traditional powers have been delegated to circle officers and other gazetted officers. The other reforms Assam has initiated include holding weekly cabinet meetings in different districts to let the ministers understand the problems of the citizens in every district and the state at large, thus enabling the cabinet to formulate district-specific policies, if required.

The different policies and administrative measures of various states are being shared between them to expedite rapid economic, technological and infrastructural development of the districts, and to minimize their wide disparities, enabling them to be at par with each other. Modi had initiated these reforms during his chief ministerial tenure, involving civil servants, elected representatives and citizens.

Modi, however, has been charged with compromising on collective governance, breaking protocols, subordinating his ministerial colleagues, elevating the ranks of his top officials in the PMO, and centralizing the powers of the cabinet in the office of the PM, as in the form of the American presidency. These traits, it is alleged, have existed since he became a chief minister. Cabinet meetings used to be over in ten minutes. Afterwards, he used to interact informally with the ministers, if the need arose. He preferred to work with civil servants and experts, and seek suggestions from citizens.

In search of rapid development, he constantly looks forward to innovative methods—administrative and technological policies—which brings him in constant touch with diverse innovators. He consults them and coordinates with them to overcome diverse obstacles and vested interests. The constant innovations and the responsibilities of his chair make him a leader who works with the team. In the party or the Sangh, even when he was not the chief minister, he worked with a team. Always being open to new ideas, persuading others to embrace his ideas, helping in reconciliations in case of differences within the organization, taking responsibility with autonomy, fixing targets, and formulating policies and overseeing their application have been his hallmarks. Essentially a team man but also the leader of the team, it's a role achieved through hard work, innovation and dedication, which has made him the fulcrum of the government.

His office, the PMO, has correspondingly become the fulcrum of administration. In fact, there is already a suggestion to make it equal and complementary to the cabinet secretariat, or to merge it with the cabinet secretariat 'into one entity'.[16] Rapid reforms require the speedy application of big ideas at national and international scale, for which the basic structure of administration and rules need updating, through redrafting or refining the Allocation of Business (AOB) Rules of 1961.

As authority has politically shifted from the cabinet to the PM, accountability has also shifted. Correspondingly, the PMO, as a result, has become the last word on administration. Technically, it exists to provide secretarial assistance to the PM, but since Shastri's time, new roles have been added to its functions; it was the role of the policy advisor and monitor that resulted in making the PMO a coordinator, influencer and instructor.[17]

In contrast, the technical role of the cabinet secretariat remains unchanged; its political-administrative importance, however, has declined under the one-party dominant governments. The principal secretaries already chair the interdepartmental meetings for the application of the reform agendas, making the cabinet secretariat as the fulcrum of administration passé.

Therefore, the allegations surrounding Modi are bereft of any knowledge of the historical trajectory of the PMO and the office of the PM, which had already acquired a prime ministerial form during Nehru's time, as discussed earlier, and which is the global trend most visible in the Canadian polity, akin to India.

Comparison: England, Canada and Australia

The role and size of the PMO in India has changed in the past 75 years. A similar change is noticeable in Canada, Australia and Britain in different proportions. Slowest to this change is England; in the other three countries including India, changes have been comparatively faster. A little resistance from the political, academic, bureaucratic and journalistic segments is noticeable in these three countries. However, these have not posed any major obstacles to the evolving powers of the PMO, which reflects the 'presidentializing' powers of the PM, and the universalizing trend of the centralization of executive powers in parliamentary democracies. Here, it will be apt to analyze the changing powers of the PMO in the three Commonwealth countries—Britain, Canada and Australia—to compare and understand the changes in India.

England

Let's begin with England, which has bequeathed its form of administrative and political rule on these three countries of the Commonwealth at the time of transfer of power during the decolonization process. England itself has witnessed the slowest growth in the expansion of the powers of the PMO, whereas the other three have witnessed faster growth. While Attlee, the British PM, felt that the PM must reflect on the procedure of the administration, including the collective voices of his cabinet, his party, and the 'country as a whole' to reach a consensus,[1] the prime ministers of India, Canada and Australia have made different practical applications of these organizations, leading to the prime ministerial-presidential form of government.

In England, except for the period of Margaret Thatcher and Tony Blair, changes have been extremely slow to come in, in terms of the powers of the prime ministers. The resignation of a senior minister could 'destabilize the prime minister'[2]. Thatcher and Blair, however, as stated earlier, 'accelerated the decline of the cabinet, reducing the frequency and duration of meetings.'[3] This is because cabinet meetings symbolize the collegiality of decision-making. 'Under old school prime ministers, full cabinet met once and often twice a week,'[4] and the meetings lasted for two to four hours. In the Thatcher-Blair era, it was reduced to thirty to forty minutes to complete the constitutional procedure, for it was considered a waste of time.

The focus was more on the cabinet committees or the informal bilateral meetings between the cabinet ministers and the PM. These committees or informal bilateral meetings gradually shifted power in a sublime way towards the prime ministerial form. 'When Margaret Thatcher sought advice, it was not about what to do but about how to implement decisions to which she was committed…[she] often compelled ministers to go along with her by force of personality…[and] threat to ministerial careers.'[5] This is when the PMO acquired more powers. The ministers' powers were undermined; each cabinet minister was regularly called upon by the PM to monitor the progress of the works of different ministries. The staff of the PMO attended these meetings 'to make sure each oar is being pulled as it should.'[6] David Miliband, part of the Blair team, argued in his defence that cabinets met 'when governments were factionalized and divided.'[7] In other words, to him, the cabinet did not represent collegiality or the collective. It represented a coalition of diverse interests, compelling collective negotiations under the rubric of the cabinet, which was 'far from the Platonic idea of [a] Cabinet government.'[8]

There is wide agreement among the reading public that there is a decline of the cabinet, which has been replaced by the prime ministerial form, accelerated by the tenures of Thatcher and Blair. A discordant view, however, is that if prime ministers are let off the leash of the cabinet system, they may be ejected by the cabinet and the party, which has been seen in the past. The majority of prime ministers in the past 75 years have worked within the system, bending it partially through creating a sub-system of cabinet committees. The members of these committees are decided by the PM. Blair was charged for being 'bossy'; however, he defended himself by stating that he 'gives a lead'. It is the majority strength of the party in the House of Commons that may influence the functioning of the PM. Tony Benn has summed up the development of the past 75 years:

'Clem (Attlee) was very collective in character… Wilson was very much a committee man… Jim (Callaghan) was an old trade unionist who believed you ought to discuss… And now we have the president.'[9]

Benn termed the Thatcher-Blair era as a presidential form of functioning, a similar term that has been used in the Canadian academic discourse. Earlier, Attlee had argued that 'he is only the first among equals… His voice will carry the greatest weight. But he can't ride rough-shod over a Cabinet.'[10] Thatcher, on the contrary, wanted to take all the decisions, as remarked by Rob Butler who was once part of Thatcher's team. Attlee recommended and changed the functioning of the cabinet to the committee system in his long association with the government in different capacities. Thatcher changed it to a presidential form by widening her PMO 'with a well-equipped and diversified staff to work out the main lines of [a] plan which [was] to be implemented in the departments.'[11] Attlee had also recommended the development of a cohesive cabinet secretariat headed by a cabinet secretary as part of the machinery of the government, to make it efficient in the application of its policies. He did not recommend the development of the PMS either when he was the chancellor, postmaster general, leader of the opposition, deputy PM or the PM. He preferred consensus in the cabinet over imposing his views, as was adopted later by Thatcher.

Churchill and Macmillan were equally collegial in their functioning. Churchill, however, kept the nuclear agenda secret from the cabinet. Macmillan felt that cabinet meetings had become so formal—as the minutes of the meetings were recorded—that one could not express oneself freely. Earlier, MacDonald had appointed a press secretary and Baldwin had appointed a career civil servant as PPS. Prior to him, the PM's secretariat was a 'private office' with non-civil servant appointees. In the 1990s, Blair appointed a chief of staff; the cabinet secretary privately advised him against it. As a result, the chief of staff remained, but a new PPS was also appointed. This arrangement has continued since then with intermittent changes.

The progression in the method of governance in the past 200 years in the British democracy has been from the collective mode of parliament to cabinet to prime ministerial form, where the chief executive has the dominant say, and leads and coordinates.

In fact, 'some decisions are taken by the prime minister alone… The prime minister stands at the apex, supported by and giving power to a widening series of rings of senior ministers, the cabinet, its committees, non-cabinet ministers and departments.'[12]

And the reasons for this change are the incremental shifts in power relations, with the PM's role involving a wide range of activites, such as chairing the cabinet and its committees, managing the relationship between the monarch and the cabinet, the selection and removal of ministers, and the appointment of senior officers, ecclesiastical heads, institutional heads, professors at the Oxford and Cambridge universities, as well as the allocation of ministries, not least being the leader of the House.

Such power relations were best reflected in Thatcher's government. She had selected her cabinet 'to advice and assist her', for she did not believe her policies should be voted down by them. Unlike her predecessors, she did not believe in consensus and dialogue, considering them a waste of time. John Major, her successor, returned to the pre-Thatcher style of functioning of collegiality in the cabinet and partly dismantled the edifice of the PMO. Arguments and discussions were allowed; questions were raised and everyone had the chance to speak; but it was a temporary phase.

With the arrival of Tony Blair as the new PM, it was once again 'Blair, Blair, Blair, just as it was Thatcher, Thatcher, Thatcher.'[13] He was no longer *primus inter pares*; he was above that: a Caesar, a Colossus. The two—Blair and Thatcher—tried to construct a 'command premiership'. The old model of the cabinet was dead; it was no longer collegial. It was the Policy Unit, the Strategic Communication Unit and the Research and Information Unit in the PMO which advised on policymaking and played the dominant role in the government. When anxious questions were raised about it in the parliament, it was assured that there was no violation of any constitutional provision. Only the scale of the advisory role and the number of advisors had changed. The Policy Unit had grown from eight under Major to 14 under Blair. Another four worked within the Private Office, and 10 others were in Communications. One was in the Research and Information Unit as a psephologist and political analyst.[14] Then there was the Social Exclusion Unit and the Performance and Innovation Unit. The Blair government was mockingly charged for being a government of units, and in effect being an expansion of Thatcher's style of functioning.

The government defended the units in the PMO as synchronized coordination between the PMO and the cabinet secretariat. In subsequent years, the scale of the staff and the units in the PMO were brought down, but their roles remained intact. The reversal to the old, collegial mode or the downscaling of the role of policy units was more due to the personalities of the cabinet and the functioning style of the PM. There is also pressure from different institutions such as the parliament, the press, the parties, and the long traditions of the modern democratic process, which force the PM to return to the collegial system. Within the cabinet and ruling party, members are not willing to accept a command premiership; and opposition to it has grown over the course of time, despite a general trend of growth of the prime ministerial form of government over the decades. This has slowed down or reversed command premiership, resulting in restraints on the PMO. In 1945, when Churchill lost the elections, his statistical section in the PMO with 20 staff members comprising economists and compilers, created during the war, was dismantled. Attlee's creation of a post of a permanent press secretary, however, remains till date.

Earlier, till the First World War, cabinet meetings were informal and the PM himself took notes. The appointment of a private secretary to the prime minister, to fix appointments or look after the correspondence, began only in 1868. Till then, these tasks were done by the PM himself. Gladstone and then Disraeli began and continued with the appointment. Disraeli appointed the first PPS out of his staff of three, and in his last term, Gladstone appointed West, a retired civil servant, as his first chief of staff. But it was David Lloyd George who formally established the PMS and the cabinet secretariat after 1916, during the First World War, to smoothen the administration through coordination. However, the two were not policy advisory bodies.

After Lloyd George, the PMS was abolished by his successor, Law. Baldwin, however, brought it back and it was subsequently consolidated. But then the ministers began to retaliate with their complaints against the PMS. The appointment of Hurd as the political secretary to PM Edward Heath in 1968, with access to papers, and the creation of a policy unit by PM Wilson in 1974 began the institutionalized damage to the collegial functioning of the cabinet.[15] One of the side effects was an increase in the number of staff members and another was their intervention in the functioning of other departments. Overall there has been a definitive change towards the prime ministerial form. The degree of it, however, depends on the operative style of the incumbent. Different prime ministers have different styles of functioning, despite a similar nature of work, lending to the centralization of powers.

Canada

In Canada, the development of the prime ministerial form has been much faster in comparison. The academia there is overwhelmingly concerned with presidentializing the form of prime ministerial functioning. The cabinet as an institution survives, like the parliament, but its effective collegial powers have been dented with the rise of the prime minister's power since 1968, when Pierre Trudeau was the PM. Mulroney, Chretien and others later strengthened it. 'The result is that important decisions are no longer made in Cabinet.'[16] The major decisions are taken in the PMO, the Privy Council Office, and with the provincial prime ministers. Policy decisions taken without prior cabinet consultations are usually due to their politically sensitive nature, or when there is no consensus, the final decision rests with the PM. The PM usurps the prerogative. Interestingly, cabinet ministers are supportive of powerful PMs. It is justified as a requirement, but it is to be used wisely.

Consequently, this led to the PMO enjoying wide-ranging powers, and the departments being brought along to work in coordination with it. The PMO briefs the PM before every cabinet meeting. In the cabinet, the PM listens to the ministers, but the final decision rests with the PM, which is shaped by the ideas of the advisers in the PMO. In the cabinet, civil servants rarely speak unless asked to by the PM; or they speak while presenting their technical reports. The cabinet and its committees meet regularly; there are open discussions and the PM sums up the meetings. Many times, ministers are reluctant to speak, particularly the new ones, and rarely express dissent. Many times, the prime ministers do not trust their cabinet colleagues, and do not delegate departmental committee powers to them. Colleagues in the committee are the ones who are trusted.

Political discourse tends to agree that the prime ministerial form of governance exists; but there are institutionalized cabinet meetings and departmental autonomy in decision-making. Functionally, it is a hybrid of collegial and individual traits. But in the last 50 years, the collegial mode has receded to the background; it has been replaced gradually by the prime ministerial form. 'Unelected officials are playing an increasing role in executive governance... Ministers are feeling more pressure from the Prime Minister's office and the Privy Council Office.'[17]

In 1980, Joe Clark, who was once the PM, delivered a lecture that summed up the development of the prime ministerial form. He joined the office with a determination to undo the centralization of the powers of the PM, which was undermining the cabinet representing the pluralistic views of Canada. The institutional change he initiated gave considerable power to the internal committees of the cabinet. He ordered the officers of the Privy Council to report to the committees while keeping the PM informed.[18] He decentralized power to the cabinet through its committees and consulted different experts from the list of government advisors to understand their perspectives and inputs on policymaking. Clark argued that the PM must not remain confined to one perspective or view; rather, his views must be democratized through widening the consultative process to incorporate different views for a national policy.

As the control of the parliament over the government has weakened over the years, due to the formation of the government of the majority party—which in turn is controlled by the political executive in the government—the daily accountability of the

PM towards the citizens, or the control of the citizens over the government, has weakened. Clark endorsed in the public domain that parliamentary accountability and control (over the government) had broken down in Canada to the point where, for all practical purposes, it did not exist, resulting in making the PM far more powerful than it was originally envisaged.[19] Clark felt that for national legitimacy and the representation of plural views, the parliament and the cabinet needed to act as checks on the PM and on his inner cabinet, committees and advisors, due to the fact that he commands the premiership through these mechanisms, apart from being the leader of the ruling party in the parliament.

In his lecture, Clark was responding to the situation in Canada that had emerged in the 1970s and 1980s, when Francophone Quebec felt alienated from the Canadian state and sought separation. For the legitimacy of the Canadian state, visibly represented by the PM, the co-optation of Quebec's views was essential for unity. Thus, when Clarke became the PM, he gave due importance to Quebec representatives in his cabinet and administration. He argued that Canada must not be run from the singular perspective of the PM and his advisors. It was diversity that created constitutional and political federalism. To respect this diversity, and for legitimacy, the cabinet must be effectively collegial and diverse. He felt that the prime ministerial form of functioning, both at the federal and provincial levels, was 'fundamentally fatal to the idea of provincial powers…and to the idea of [the] federal system.'[20] This form of presidentializing the powers for efficient and effective governance was not required. Pluralism and democratic functioning could be equally effective and efficient while simultaneously providing popular legitimacy to the rule.

John Courtney, however, felt that in the executive branches of democracy—parliamentary and presidential—a phenomenon of advisor and bureau had cropped up, which was common across the forms. The difference was that while in the parliamentary system there was an opportunity and mechanisms to have alternative advisory opinions, in the presidential form there was a strong possibility of a singular advisory perspective that could have a devastating effect.[21] These unelected advisors embedded in the prime ministerial form become a 'class' in themselves to protect their interests. The phenomenon that began with Trudeau has, over the years, marginalized the control of the parliament and the cabinet over the PM. The changes carried out 'in the rules of the parliament and in the organization of the executive' have been 'altered significantly'. Courtney, however, felt that 'the functions of the prime minister had been spelled out in [the] Cabinet minute which remains to this day the definitive statement of the prime minister's special prerogatives,'[22] which was transferred in *transitu* from Britain during the transfer of power in 1867.

As the responsibilities of the PM have evolved, so have the powers of the executive been transferred to the PM. Some of the special prerogatives are the dissolution of the parliament, the appointment of a chief justice of the courts, recommending the appointment of the governor-general, privy councillors, lieutenant governors, the speaker of the senate, and many others. The list of powers is for both appointments and recommendations. The concluding argument is that this list of powers rests upon a person 'whose position and office are not referred to in Canada's written constitution'. Courtney, thus, provides a different perspective on presidentializing the powers of the Canadian PM, whose office (PMO) has the largest staff (including that of the PCO and the FPRO) in comparison to Britain and America.

In 1939, after the Brownlow Committee report, America's White House Office (WHO) was reorganized in its functioning, which included 'six personal assistants, the Bureau of the Budget (transferred from the Treasury) and institutions for planning, personal management...[it] includes the President's closet personal advisers who control the all-important access to the President...[its] four critical functions [are] to keep the president's finger on the pulse of the native through professional public relations advisors; to brief the president on the activities and problems of the executive departments and agencies...to act as liaison between the executive branch and the legislative branch...to advise the president on military matters and national security.'[23] This organizational structure and its functions are at the discretion of the president, unlike the functioning and structure of the thirteen executive departments, which need the approval of the Congress. The chief of staff heads the office, followed by assistants to the President Counsel, the Speaker of the Senate or those of equivalent rank. Their primary roles are to provide inputs, judgement, analyses and infrastructure to the president to help him to take decisions. Their average tenure, not of the inner circle, is of two years, working 10 to 12 hours a day, five and a half days a week. The nature of work is intense. 'The recruitment is done on an informal and personal basis...who is known and trusted...[usually], a background investigation is conducted...for security reasons.'[24] The staff is physically located in the West Wing of the White House and in the Old Executive Office building.

The White House staff enjoys more political clout than the cabinet members. Jimmy Carter attempted to restore the supremacy of the cabinet in his initial years. But after two and a half years, the White House staff once again regained dominance.

This trend is equally visible in the prime ministerial form of government. Canada under Pierre Trudeau, since 1968, has gradually witnessed it. The PMO is located in Langevin Block, Ottawa, which also has the Privy Council Office (PCO). Their combined power has grown over the years. It was reflected in a survey conducted to find out the level of the prime ministerial form in different countries, where Canada had the highest rating, followed by Australia and Britain.[25] The cabinet is known as a committee of different members who discuss issues without the powers of budgetary approvals. The decisions are taken in the PMO and the cabinet approves them and the ministry of finance funds them. It's the PM who is responsible for a unified programme, legislation and application. Before 1987, the PS headed the PMO. After 1987, it became the chief of staff who heads the office. Its primary roles are to act as a political arm between the government and the party, be the policy-advisor to the PM, act as a strategist, write speeches, and work with the PCO (equivalent to cabinet secretariat) to execute government decisions. The PCO, headed by a civil servant, is the official advisor to the PM, as it is the top executive wing of the administration. Paul Martin changed the structure of the PMO to match the WHO, the executive office of the president of the USA.

There is an interesting argument in academia that compares the prime ministerial form with the American presidency, which is fallacious. For the political support the PM enjoys in the parliament is rarely enjoyed by the American president; the American president would rather prefer to be the PM of either Australia or Canada with their PMOs. Equating the functioning style of the PM to that of the president is superficial. These are two different systems with their strength and shortcomings that have evolved over decades against an anti-colonial backdrop. The two have their diverse procedures and legalese, and with a change in the context, new operational ways are emerging among different forms of political executives across the countries.

Another interesting perspective is that 'the dynamics of the party make collective cabinet essential because otherwise a prime minister finds himself at odds… Since 1925, all Canadian leaders have been elected by Convention… The only way a Canadian prime minister can be removed is through the calling of a leadership convention and vote of no confidence.'[26] The PM, therefore, is forced to consult his colleagues in the cabinet, the party and different segments of the electorate. What is known as the prime ministerial/presidential form is essentially the operating style of an individual. The democratic-consultative-collective form continues into the policymaking process. The clerical work which the PM used to do at an earlier stage, like writing the minutes of the cabinet, is now done by his PMO, and the coordination work of the meetings is handled by the office.

Two parallel trends can be observed. One, with the democratization of society, parties are also becoming more democratic. The prime ministerial candidates of parties are, therefore, democratically elected in leadership conventions. Two, the clerical-advisory works are delegated more to professional groups for practical application and efficient execution. The argument thus posits that the operating style of the prime ministers should not be confused with a lack of collective functioning and concentration of power with them. In a federation like Canada, the cabinet is equally representative of the different provinces. An oversight of it may lead to a political-electoral backlash in the party leadership convention, and in the general/provincial elections. This democratization of the political process forces the PM to look to the collective for decision-making. A third perspective is the reverse. It argues that the cabinet itself has evolved out of the legislature, which is the larger collective with wider representation. The cabinet has usurped the power of the legislature and is more a form of centralized powers of administration and governance bestowed on a narrow body of a few ministers. The prime ministerial form is a further centralization of power in one person. His election is democratic, both at the party and electoral levels, but the powers in him are centralized. This is a unique, contradictory trend, but it is a balance between the democratic and administrative requirements of contemporary times. Professional efficiency in the administrative application of decisions in combination with a democratic consultative process in different evolving forms is the need of the hour.

Australia

In Australia, there are different interpretations of the prime ministerial form of government. In comparison to Canada, there is less centralization of powers in the PMO. In comparison to Britain, however, it is more.[27] This was the conclusion of a survey of experts in which the powers of the prime ministers were analyzed in different countries of the world which follow the Westminster system. Constitutionally, the PMO in Australia is not mentioned. Yet, what has emerged in Australia is considered to be a prime ministerial form, despite the limitations imposed by the federal system, which restrain the PM from taking decisions in many areas.

There is an interesting case of PM Billy Hughes, unique in itself, who ran the government of England for 15 months during 1918–19. Secretarial assistance in the form of the PMO itself evolved from non-existence. Subsequently, the Department of the PM and Cabinet (PM&C) also evolved. Earlier, 'the prime minister used to keep the minutes; he used to write down on one side of the minute book the topics…the people who turned up and the decisions…but gradually the prime ministers [started] formalizing the process of government.'[28]

Since 1939, secretarial staff began to sit in cabinet meetings to record the minutes. In the past 85 years, the bureaucracy has grown more complex. Today, the PMO is a private office that provides political advice and executive assistance. It is headed by the chief of staff, who may not be a professional civil servant. Earlier, before 1972, the PMO was headed by the PPS who used to be a career civil servant. The PMO now is packed with party advisers, media specialists, political strategists and a national security advisor. It coordinates with the ministries, private businesses and non-state actors and provides advice to the PM. Furthermore, it coordinates the application of the decisions taken by the government. The PMO was created by Malcom Fraser and subsequently expanded by Bob Hawke, Paul Keatings and John Howard. It was Whitlam who created the designation of chief of staff in 1972 and changed its composition and role. Earlier, its role was to provide secretarial assistance to the PM.

The PM&C is the cabinet secretariat which assists the PM and the cabinet or its committees in routine administrative and procedural work. It coordinates the ministerial portfolio and advises the PM on cabinet matters. Actually, earlier it was the cabinet secretary who was the official advisor to the PM and the cabinet. As the PM acquired greater political and media prominence, more expectations from the electorate and responsibilities fell on his shoulders. He began to have a greater say in decision-making, which, he felt, needed professional advice. The separation and development of the PMO from the cabinet secretariat is the result of this political electoral development, in which the leadership conventions of the parties, their prime ministerial candidates, and fierce electoral contests have played important roles. The two visible contradictory trends of democratization and centralization are being propelled by global capitalism and mass movements. They are forcing a national government towards presidentializing the powers of the executive while simultaneously democratizing societies and delegating powers. It restrains the executive from becoming dictatorial; rather, it compels it to be democratic and representational in functioning.

The cabinet meets regularly. It has its committees, issues are discussed, ministries are consulted, and procedures are followed, despite the pre-ordained decisions of the prime ministers on many of the issues in consultation with the PMO, private businesses and the party. Patrick Weller feels that collective governance in Australia is still much more prominent than elsewhere. The cabinet government to him is 'an arena, not a set of rules... It's a process by which people work to establish a coherent set of policies consistent with its strategic directions. It's the place where the political, the policy and the administrative interests intersect.'[29]

As the first minister, the PM's role has also evolved over a century to fit into the changing context of the times. The formation of the National Security Council, the expenditures review committee and the war cabinet has been the initiative of the prime minister. Weller gives a series of examples to demonstrate that the earlier prime ministers were equally powerful and that there was not much centralization/presidentialization of powers. In fact, he is loath to accept the term and argues that there have been only operational changes as per the personality of the PM and the requirements of changing times. Of course, media visibility has increased manifold, which creates an impression regarding the growing powers of the PM. It has also generated much political and public pressure on him to deliver quickly and correctly, to the satisfaction of the larger national community. Finally, it has resulted in constant growth of professional advisors and secretarial assistants over the past hundred years.

There was a time when nine cabinet ministers used to discuss issues around a table without any papers, and the PM himself used to write the minutes. But there was also a Cabinet Committee in 1903 which was far ahead of the introduction of the committee system in Britain. Weller thus concludes with the point that different prime ministers have introduced different methods of working as suited to their politics, personality and the requirements of the time. The cabinet has remained since its introduction in 1901. It has been a political and policy forum where contests and consultation are ongoing. The moot point is to find out why this collective decision-making process is still functional.

One reason is that Australia is a federal country. The federal cabinet has representations from the different provinces. To keep the electoral dynamics of their constituencies alive, ministers representing their provinces contest for larger allocations of resources for their provinces, and that leads to consultation and collective decision-making. The tradition among the parties to democratically elect their leaders leads to a series of accommodations. The absence of consensus, consultation and collective decision-making may create challenges for the PM. The advisory support to the prime minister from his private office creates an impression that there is a prime ministerial form of government. Since prime ministerial candidates are a creation of the parties and leadership conventions, it is built into the system that a PM will consult the cabinet and take decisions collectively, lest he faces challenges within the party and disruptions in the electoral mobilization for legislative dominance in the formation of the government.

The Department of the PM was formed in 1911 to assist in the administrative requirements of the cabinet. Before it, the office of the Ministry of External Affairs was used for secretarial work, as the PM was also concurrently the minister of external affairs. In 1968, John Gorton created a separate section out of it to serve the cabinet exclusively. The other section which served the PM exclusively was re-modified in 1972 as the PMO. Its function was modified to provide political and other advice to the PM. The cabinet secretariat focused purely on giving administrative advice and support to the cabinet and the PM. The secretary was a civil servant who headed operations; he was analogous to the cabinet secretary. The PMO was headed by the PPS. Later, the post was renamed as chief of staff, and the appointee was no longer required to be a career civil servant. The PPS was a civil servant. As the role of the PMO changed, so did the composition of its staff and the designation of its head. While the cabinet secretariat looked after the formation and application of the four major categories of policies, the PMO provided complete support—political, media and others—to the PM as required. So, from the Department of the PM to the PM&C to the PMO, it has been a long journey.

Actually, there is mutual interdependence between the PM and his cabinet colleagues. 'Ministers depend on the prime minister for support in getting funds from Finance. In turn, the prime minister depends on his ministers to deliver the party's electoral promises.'[30] Cooperation in the party and the government is an equally important component of mutual interdependence. The pluralization of advice, even if critical, is always a welcome act. As the cabinet is a legal requirement in the Westminster model, it is imperative for a PM to follow the procedure. The committee system, the bilateral style of functioning of the PM, or the media optics do not do away with the imperatives of electoral politics and party requirements of teamwork; and teamwork always demands collective decision-making. So even if a PM may prefer the presidentialization of power, executive coordination propels the requirement of collegial functioning. The absence of it, and the personalization of party and government leadership, may sink the PM in electoral contests. On the other hand, a pack of yes-men in the government and in the party is equally bad for the PM. The electoral contest thus demands that a PM have capable leaders in the party and in the government, with whom he can discuss policies and executive coordination conjointly; the federal structure is another systemic dynamo that makes the cabinet functioning an imperative. A domineering leadership style may isolate a PM from both the party and the cabinet.

From Barton, in 1901, who focused on white Australia and universal suffrage in his election campaign, to Morrison, the contemporary PM, there have been debates on the decline of collegial functioning, and on the growth of the presidentialization of the powers of the PM. In substance, there has not been much change. In form, in the operational style of prime ministers, there have been changes. But this has existed since early times. What has been changing is the office of the PMO and of the cabinet secretariat for offering secretarial assistance and policy advice to the PM and to the cabinet. The expansion of the role of the PMO has created an image in the public domain that there has been an expansion of prime ministerial power. While a few administrative powers of appointment or recommendatory powers have definitely been bestowed upon him, largely these are to be approved by the cabinet.

Summing up

In the three countries of the Commonwealth, namely Britain, Canada and Australia, there are similarities in the functioning of the PMO and the cabinet secretariat as the latter two countries follow the Westminster model. Both offices have evolved over the decades. The PM was earlier dependent on the cabinet secretariat for advisory and secretarial assistance. From the 1970s onwards, the prime ministers in the three countries had their own elaborate PMO with analogous powers of the cabinet secretariat. They also empowered their PMOs to assist them in their political-electoral and publicity works.

As the contests for the party-prime ministerial leadership became more organized, the parties began to hold leadership conventions. The candidates who emerged victorious and won the elections were bestowed with more responsibilities, leading to a more personality-centric functioning in the party, and in the government. The change emerged as a systemic requirement and to match the ambition-driven style of the prime ministers. But the consultations and suggestions of colleagues would also be taken into account. These developments in the past 50 years have created two major interpretations in the academic-public discourse: while one school talks of a prime ministerial-presidential form of government, the other school talks of a collegial form. Both, however, agree that there are differences in the functioning of the PMO. While the first school argues 'that the prime minister is more powerful than the Cabinet because he or she is the leader of the party, has the power to appoint and dismiss ministers, chairs the Cabinet and controls its agenda...,' the other school argues that 'the party cannot be ignored...ministers have their own bases of support...Constitutional Conventions require the government to act collectively...'[31]

The fact remains that in cabinet meetings, it is the PM who carries his policies forward as a collegial decision in the garb of summing up the discussions. It is equally important that prime ministers carry their colleagues. In case of a rebellion of important colleagues, the political longevity of the prime ministers can come under threat. Tenures of many prime ministers, including Thatcher, have been cut short due to this. Usually, such situations arise when prime ministerial predominance is demonstrated in three ways: by a general domineering style to decide policy across all issues, in key areas, and in predicting hard solutions to most policy problems.[32] This curtails the freedom of manoeuvrability and limits the political space of the ministers, which may jeopardize their political-electoral future. It further makes them dependent on the prime ministers, which may curtail their independent, individual identity. In order to lessen the competition, prime ministers do such acts wilfully. The PMO provides institutional support as it initiates and coordinates the works of the party and the administration. The more domineering the prime minister, the greater is the role of the PMO. The cabinet secretariat gets reduced to doing procedural works: drawing up the agenda of the cabinet, processing departmental submissions, keeping the cabinet minutes, recording its conclusions, circulating them to departments, and trying to ensure they are implemented.[33]

In India, Canada and Australia, the PMO has the larger domineering role. In the pre-Thatcher years in England, the cabinet played the domineering role. In the Thatcher-Blair years, the PMO acquired a more important position. Subsequently, the position of the cabinet secretariat has been largely restored. In the last 50 years, the development has been more towards the importance of the PMO. It has, however, been argued with a contrarian perspective that a weak person needs a powerful PMO to carry forward his agenda with the institutional support of his private/departmental office. A strong personality does not require such support; rather, he gets his administrative works done through the office of the cabinet secretariat. As the cabinet secretariat cannot be used for political purposes, prime ministers use the PMO instead. In all four countries, this has been the trend for the past 50 years. Britain was the last to join it in the Thatcher-Blair years. In the other three countries, such developments have been around since the 1960s.

Unfortunately, the popular perception created through the political-media discourse is that the prime ministers who strengthened the PMO and used it as a political tool were strong persons. The divergent, plural views in policymaking can also come through the cabinet secretariat instead of through the PMO. The lateral entry of different experts through minor administrative modifications can enrich the cabinet, and thereby help check the expansion of the PMO. When prime ministers felt that they were getting only particular kinds of views from the civil servants, insufficient for a pluralized electorate, to co-opt pluralized requirements in their policies they would bring in experts in the PMO, which in turn overshadowed the cabinet secretariat.

Conclusion

In 1773, the East India Company, after seizing power in Bengal, began to work through the EC, known as the Governor-General in Council. As their territories and work expanded, members of the council were assigned particular works to look after for routine functioning, which were termed portfolios and departments. Bigger and important works of policy decisions were taken up by the council. A Joint Consultative Board of the EC was set up, headed by the private secretary of the governor-general who did two jobs: worked in the council and served as the private secretary. This structure was streamlined through the 1861 Act. The board's main work was to circulate agenda papers of meetings. Initially, the private secretary was not a part of the council meetings. Subsequently, he was brought into the meetings by the governor-general. Since 1935, he was also called the secretary to the EC. Later on, the posts were separated, and a different secretary of the EC was appointed. The EC formed a secretariat in 1945 to service the Co-ordination Committee of the War Resources and Reconstruction.[1] This became the Cabinet Secretariat[1] in September 1946, i.e. the secretary of the EC became the Cabinet Secretary. The Private Office of the Viceroy, on the other hand, became the PMS, and the Secretary of the Private Office became the Principal Private Secretary to the PMS.

Since then, over the past 75 years, the PMS-PMO has been changing both in terms of its organizational structure and its roles. During the Nehru years, there was no substantive change in it. What he altered, in praxis, was the functioning of the PM.

His cabinet colleagues no longer remained equal; he changed the status of the PM from *primus inter pares* to the boss, while the cabinet members became his aides and advisors rather than being ministers at par with him. It transformed the nature of the government, and the style of its functioning, from cabinet to prime ministerial. Later on, Shastri institutionalized it through the structure of the PMS, empowered it with the advisory role, including policy initiatives, and elevated the secretary of the PMS to the rank of cabinet secretary.

The cabinet secretariat and the ministries became subordinate to the PMS as files began to be sent to the PMS for their prior clearance or approval. Earlier, during Patel's time, or even after his death, it was not a routine matter, which it became in subsequent years. In Desai's time as well, files were not sent to the PMO for prior approval of the PM. For coordination among the ministries, it was the cabinet secretariat which did the job, not the PMS; and it was from the cabinet that prior approval for any policy initiative by any ministry was required, not from the PM. During the Indira Gandhi-Rajiv Gandhi years, however, prior approval of the PMS-PMO was the acceptable norm. The process, in an embryonic form, began during the Shastri years. Therefore, a system of ghost files in the PMO, parallel to the files that came from ministries, was created. The mechanism was devised by the PMS during the Shastri years to subvert the supreme hierarchy of the cabinet while keeping the facade of official procedure intact. This resulted in the administrative subversion of official hierarchy.

Files sent by the cabinet office/ministries were not sent to the PM directly. These were marked for the joint secretaries who then obtained orders from the secretary of the PMS. The PM would then see the shadow notes recorded by the PMS. Consequently, this meant that the cabinet secretary no longer remained the chief advisor to the PM, with the status of being the sole custodian of the advisory power representing the cabinet secretariat. Its domain was now shared by the PMS, represented by the principal secretary/secretary. This change was executed through administrative orders which unofficially altered the relationship between the PM and his cabinet colleagues, and between the PMO and the cabinet secretariat. The constitutional position, however, remained unaltered, and the procedure remained the same.

The tenure of Haksar as secretary and then as PS, who was one of the long-serving officers in the PMS, subsequently followed by P.C. Alexander, T.K.A. Nair, Brajesh Mishra, Nripendra Mishra and P.K. Mishra, further pushed the cabinet secretary to officialese. It no longer remained the office of power, desire and awe. Its exclusive domain was substituted by the PMS, which was the new centre of power where officers were chosen by the PM or were appointed on the recommendation of senior officers in the PMS. The official climbing up in the bureaucratic hierarchy was no longer a pre-requisite to join it, as many of the principal secretaries were retired officers. The appointment of retired civil servants as the PS, and elevating their rank to the level of minister, were some other subversions of the cabinet secretariat.

Unfortunately, this trend became the standard operating feature of the prime ministers. Only Charan Singh took the initiative of abolishing the post of the PS and appointed a serving officer as his secretary. Rajiv Gandhi, too, thought of doing away with it after the exit of Alexander. He therefore delayed the appointment of Sarla Grewal, and instead brought in parliamentary secretaries to expedite the works of development, without going through the labyrinth of officialese. But this failed. Earlier, starting from Desai, the other prime ministers continued with the procedure that Indira Gandhi had initiated for Haksar. Then, when she came back to power in January 1980, she restored the post of PS and appointed P.C. Alexander to it. Subsequent prime ministers continued with this system, elevating the PS rank to the level of cabinet minister. From joint secretary to secretary to cabinet secretary, this development was a quantum jump in the bureaucracy within a short span.

The post has now jumped from the rank of cabinet secretary to cabinet minister, though the principal secretary gets the pay scale of the cabinet secretary, which is presently Level 18, while the secretary is on Level 17. This change in the rank of principal secretary speaks for the changing relationship of the PM with his cabinet colleagues. He no longer remains only the *primus inter pares*, but rather becomes the fulcrum of the government, and the PMO becomes the fulcrum of administration. The arguments that Nehru had posited to Gandhi to run the prime ministerial government, and the PMS that he had envisaged for himself while being in the interim government, have become a reality.

The cabinet functions, in a true sense, only when the prime ministers are new to the chair or there are coalition governments formed after the election, in the absence of a single-party majority in the Lok Sabha. In both cases, there have been multiple strong deterrences to the prime ministerial form. In the first case, the learning curve of the new job tends to make the person open to new ideas, which lets the cabinet assert itself. In the second case, it is the compulsion of the coalition that asserts collective functioning. As a result, prime ministers are not able to select their own ministries; ministers are selected by party presidents whose parties form the coalition governments; moreover, the portfolios to be given to the ministers are negotiated. It is not the free choice of the prime ministers. The number of ministers from a party is also negotiated; again, it is not the free choice of the prime ministers. The ministers, therefore, are under the command of the party presidents; and most importantly, the PM himself is chosen by the party presidents forming the coalition governments, as someone with no prior approval of the electorate as a prime ministerial candidate.

The parties/alliances that put forth to the electorate their prime ministerial candidates, for example the BJP/NDA, have better authoritative standing in the coalition government. The political stature of the PM, with a long background of political reckoning, is another important factor. Yet, in the absence of a single-party majority government, the functioning of the cabinet has been more democratic, as the decision-making has been more collegial.

Constitutionally, the prime minister has only two powers, as stated earlier: one, he selects his ministers to form his government, and second, he reports the decisions of the council of ministers to the president; it is the cabinet which takes the decisions. Even in matters of finance, as per the Transaction of Business Rules of the Government of India, the prime minister has to take the approval of the cabinet; he has the power, under Rule 12, of approval in case of urgency, but it has to be ratified by the cabinet. Being the first among equals, he chairs the cabinet meetings and the meetings of its different committees. His office, the PMO, has no special powers; neither has it any specific works assigned to it as per the Allocation of Business Rules of the Government of India, unlike other ministries and departments. It's like working in any other office of the government, with the professional competence of civil services providing secretarial assistance to prime ministers on different policies of the government, which may change with a change of government. Yet, it's not like a typical government office. There is a wide degree of flexibility in its structure, and in the nature of its work.

The prime minister can bring in any person to his office that he thinks fit for assistance in his works. But it does not become—to clarify—a party office. The PS gets the salary equivalent to that of the cabinet secretary; but when it comes to officialese, to chairing the session of the meetings of the secretaries, it is the cabinet secretary who chairs the meetings. The PS may be part of it. But usually, being of a higher or equal rank as per the Warrant of Precedence, he sends some other officer for the meeting.

The five different sections within the PMO, and the different officers heading each section, are assigned different states and ministries, to look after the works which may require the PM's attention. Many times, the initiatives of development come from the PM himself, which are communicated to the concerned ministries through notes seeking formal proposals from the ministries. Once a proposal comes in, it is scrutinized by the PMO; if found fit, it is sent to the cabinet for approval; if there is a shortcoming, the ministry is advised to redraft the proposal accordingly, as suggested by the PMO, and then send it for cabinet approval.

The PMO thus plays the role of a manufacturer, a conveyor belt, and a coordinator between the ministries and the PM. It has substantively taken over the role of the cabinet secretariat which now plays the role of a post office; on paper, however, it's the cabinet secretariat which is all-powerful, and the PMO remains an office for secretarial assistance.

This duality and dichotomy in the relationship between the PMO and the cabinet secretariat emerged after 1964. Subsequent decades strengthened it, making the PMO more powerful. Even coalition governments were not able to restore the old glory of the cabinet secretariat. Its primacy on paper, however, still remains intact.

In comparison, the change in the British PMO began in 1979, when Margaret Thatcher took over the reins of the government as PM. She created the post of the chief of staff in 1979 to initiate and seek advice on policy matters. This was unprecedented. It was the subversion of the role of the cabinet secretary and of the secretariat. Also, derivatively, it was the subversion of the role of the cabinet, which was being bypassed to institutionalize the prime ministerial form of government. Till then, the PPS headed the PMO; he was an officer of the rank of assistant secretary who provided secretarial assistance to the PM. This led to resistance from the civil services, media, cabinet ministers and parties that compelled the PM to restore the old order in 1985. Consequently, the post of the chief of staff was dismantled in 1985, and the old order was restored. In 1997, however, after a gap of 12 years, Tony Blair recreated the post. But it was once again changed. In 2007, when Gordon Brown was the PM, he changed its roles and powers; the post was not dismantled but its executive powers to direct the civil services were taken away. Only the advisory role remained with it.

Now the chief of staff reports to the cabinet secretary as he is part of the cabinet office. Earlier, for a brief period, the roles of the chief of staff and of the PPS were combined in one person, who also headed the PMO. For 16 years, during Thatcher's and Blair's tenures, the cabinet secretary and the PPS were relegated to the background. In 2011, the powers and the roles of the chief of staff were split, and two other posts were created. The cabinet secretary, however, remained the constitutional adviser of the cabinet and of the PMO. The PPS, who headed the PMO, was superseded by the chief of staff; he also superseded the cabinet secretary. Brown partially restored the old order. PM David Cameron renamed the PPS as the permanent secretary and elevated the rank of the post. Subsequently, he appointed Jeremy Heywood, who was the permanent secretary, as the cabinet secretary. Since then, the old order of the PPS was partially restored; but the chief of staff, with other posts of different advisors to the PM, remain; and the chief of staff remains a rank higher than the PPS. The power of the cabinet secretary, restored by Brown, remains as well. But his adversary in the PMO, the chief of staff with its advisory role, also remains. It reflects the curtailment of power of the cabinet secretary.

In a nutshell, the British PMS has witnessed structural changes in the past 45 years. The strengthening of the PMS was an attempt to marginalize the cabinet and strengthen the prime ministerial form. In the late 1930s, as leader of the Opposition, Attlee had recommended, and then later as PM had adopted, the committee system within the cabinet to marginalize the collective functioning of the cabinet. In India, Ambedkar had criticized Nehru for adopting such tactics to marginalize the functioning of the Indian cabinet, making its functioning more personalized and prime ministerial rather than collective.

While India moved much faster towards the prime ministerial form after the 1952 elections, the British have yet to adopt the form at such a scale. Despite attempts by many British prime ministers, there has been stiff resistance from cabinet ministers and parties, unlike in India where the transition has been comparatively smooth. It seems that there is a universal trend towards the prime ministerial form of government, which is becoming presidential in its style of functioning, without needing to amend constitutional provisions.

In Canada as well, we find a new post of chief of staff which was created in 1987 to advise the PM on policy, planning and strategies. This responsibility earlier belonged to the PCO, which has now been confined to actuate only the application of policies. The major change was enacted by PM Justin Trudeau in 1968. Before him, the role of the PS was to provide secretarial assistance, and the advisory plus executive role of application of policy was of the PCO, which is the cabinet secretariat. Now the PS is second to the chief of staff.

In all the three liberal democracies, Britain, Canada and India, there has been a major shift in the past 50 years in the functioning of prime ministers, which has led to a change in the PMO. It has become presidential in style, apparently resembling the American presidency. The PMOs, as a result, also have chiefs of staff with advisory and executive powers. In Britain, there has been stronger resistance to the prime ministerial form of functioning; therefore, changes in the PMO have been slow in comparison to Canada and India. The roles of the cabinet secretary and of the Clerk of the Privy Council (in Canada), as a result, have been marginalized; their roles have been appropriated by the chiefs of staff in Canada and Britain, and the PS in India. These functional changes, however, are without any constitutional backing. There are no amendments that alter the position of the cabinet and the PM. They remain the cabinet in form, with the PM as the *primus inter pares*. In effect, however, the *primus inter pares* has been rendered the boss, akin to the American president; and cabinet ministers have been reduced substantively, in Canada and in India, to aides or representatives of different political-social constituencies. In England, the status of the cabinet members, however, is still powerful, representing the party and the government.

The moot point now is to analyze the reasons for this change across the three countries that are similar in constitutional and governmental framework but different in social structure. While Canada and Britain are urban-industrial, India is still rural. India and Canada were British colonies that framed written Constitutions after their independence, while Britain is the earliest modern democracy with evolved conventions forming its Constitution. All three have a capitalist economy; while Canada is a modem nation-state not more than 200 years old, England and India are old societies with medieval pasts.

Diversities notwithstanding, there is a strong commonality among the three countries: the prime ministers are becoming more powerful than the cabinet. Nehru began the process in India in 1947, Trudeau in Canada in 1968, and Thatcher in Britain in 1977. The last two did it in the institutionalized way, through their PMOs, while Nehru did it informally by breaking the procedure of the functioning of the cabinet. The centralization of power in the PM is not a systemic, political or social requirement. It is more a requirement of electoral dynamics which have become much more fluid and politically competitive with changing awareness levels among citizens. Equally responsible is the personality of the prime ministerial leadership who intends to dominate the cabinet personally and politically; one of the methods is through electoral victory by leading their parties. The process adopted to remain in power, to be popular, and to be the boss is also a factor. Equally important is the perception of the electorate of their leaders that determines the private and public behaviour of their leaders. Nehru was at the helm for 17 years, Trudeau for 15 years, and Thatcher for 11 years. The last two also remained the leaders of their parties for more years than their tenures as PM. The political-psychological factors, such as having 'overriding authority' and becoming a 'supervisor', drive leaders towards the prime ministerial form. While the cabinet is collective, the prime ministerial form is individualistic. It is akin, in systemic form, to the functioning of the American presidency, whose powers fascinate the prime ministers.

The changes in the PMO, thus, are the outcome of the personal desires of the prime ministers who want to run the government as per their liking, and who do not want to formally share power with the cabinet and its secretariat for policy, planning, strategies and running the government. It has nothing to do with efficiency or requirements of security of contemporary times. Nehru's famous correspondence with Patel in 1947, cited at length earlier, on running the government as per his prerogative against the primacy of the cabinet, of which he was only the first among equals, provides the reasons for the prime ministerial form of government. More importantly, where the delivery mechanism is efficient and the party and the ministers are strong—as it happens in coalition governments—it is the cabinet that runs the government.

In a nutshell, it is a choice between the primacy of the self versus the primacy of collective governance and formally sharing power with equals. The Constitution has given the PM only two powers: to select/remove his council of ministers, and to report the decisions of the council to the president. His election as leader of the parliamentary party and the support of the electorate—in case of declaration of his prime ministerial candidature during the election—place him in a commanding position. Furthermore, the right to select his ministers and allocate their portfolios can tempt him to make the functioning of the government *de facto* prime ministerial. Therefore, Ambedkar had remarked that 'if any functioning under our constitution is to be compared with the US President, he is the prime minister.' This political-electoral placement, rather than the constitutional position, makes the PM similar to the American president in functioning. Yet, he is far away from the presidency. The multiple coalition governments amply reflect the position of the PM in India and elsewhere. One-party dominance or bi-party dominance, however, provides opportunities for the prime ministerial functioning of the government. The coalition governments are just momentary interregnums or disruptions in the process.

Annexure I

प्रधान मंत्री कार्यालय

PRIME MINISTER'S OFFICE

***

G.F. No. 402/2015-PME Dated:13th September, 2019

OFFICE ORDER

Consequent upon the appointment of Dr. P.K. Mishra as Principal Secretary to Prime Minister and Shri P.K. Sinha as Principal Advisor to Prime Minister, the Prime Minister has approved the work distribution between Principal Secretary to Prime Minister, National Security Advisor and Principal Advisor to Prime Minister as under:

(A) Principal Secretary to Prime Minister

i. Policy issues and matters relating to Ministries of Personnel, Public Grievances & Pensions and Law & Justice, Appointments Committee of the Cabinet and other appointments, Cabinet Secretariat, listing of Cabinet items, Anti-corruption Unit, PMO Establishment;

ii. All important policy issues and matters

(B) National Security Advisor (NSA)

i. Policies and matters (except appointments) relating to Ministries of External Affairs, Overseas Indian Affairs, Defence, Space, Atomic Energy, NSCN and R&AW / RAS.

ii. All policies and matters relating to NSCS, National Authority for Chemical Weapons.

iii. All matters relating to national security

(C) Principal Advisor to Prime Minister

i. Policy issues and matters relating to all Ministries / Departments / Agencies / Bodies except those specifically allocated to Principal Secretary to PM and NSA.

PRIME MINISTER'S OFFICE
(PRADHAN MANTRI KARYALAYA)

1. To provide secretarial assistance to the Prime Minister.

Annexure II

Government of India (Allocation of Business) Rules, 1961

भारत सरकार (कार्य आबंटन) नियम, 1961

(As Amended up to 31st January, 2017)

(31 जनवरी, 2017 तक यथा संशोधित)

Government of India (Allocation of Business) Rules, 1961

Index

	Subject	Pg.No.
I.	Order dated 14.01.1961	6
II.	First Schedule	8
III.	Second Schedule	13

RASHTRAPATI BHAVAN
NEW DELHI
January 14,1961/Pausa 24, 1882(S)

ORDER

THE GOVERNMENT OF INDIA (ALLOCATION OF BUSINESS) RULES

In exercise of the powers conferred by clause (3) of article 77 of the Constitution and in supercession of all previous rules and orders on the subject the President hereby makes the following rules for the allocation of the business of the Government of India.

1. Short Title - These rules may be called the Government of India (Allocation of Business) Rules, 1961.

2. Allocation of Business - The business of the Government of India shall be transacted in the Ministries, Departments, Secretariats and Offices specified in the First Schedule to these rules (all of which are hereinafter referred to as "departments").

3. Distribution of Subjects[1] –

(1) The distribution of subjects among the departments shall be as specified in the Second Schedule to these Rules and shall include all attached and subordinate offices or other organisations including Public Sector Undertakings concerned with their subjects and Sub-rules (2), (3) and (4) of this Rule.

(2) The compiling of the accounts of each Department shall stand allocated to that Department with effect from the date from which the President relieves, by order made under the first proviso to sub-section (1) of Section 10 of the Comptroller and Auditor General's (Duties, Powers and Conditions of Service) Act, 1971; the Comptroller and Auditor General from the responsibility for compiling the accounts of that Department.

(3) Where sanction for the prosecution of any person for any offence is required to be accorded-

a) If he is a Government servant, by the Department which is the Cadre Controlling authority for the service of which he is a member, and in any other case, by the Department in which he was working at the time of commission of the alleged offence;

b) If he is a public servant other than a Government servant, appointed by the Central Government, by the Department administratively concerned with the organisation in which he was working at the time of commission of the alleged offence; and

c) In any other case, by the Department which administers the Act under which the alleged offence is comitted;

Provided that where, for offences alleged to have been comitted, sanction is required under more than one Act, it shall be competent for the Department which administers any of such Acts to accord sanction under all such Acts.

---

[1] Substituted vide 116th Amendment dated 29.03.1976, thereafter, sub-para 3(1) substituted and sub-paras 3(3) and 3(4) inserted vide 187th Amendment dated 30.09.1986. Further modified vide Amendment series no.271 dated 06.01.2004.

(4) Notwithstanding anything contained in sub-rule (3), the President may, by general or special order, direct that in any case or class of cases, the sanction shall be by the Department of Personnel and Training.

Allocation of Departments among Ministers[1] –

(1) The business of the Government of India allocated to Cabinet Secretariat is and, shall always be deemed to have been, allotted to the Prime Minister. ($)

(2) Subject to the provisions of sub-rule (1), the President may, on the advise of the Prime Minister, allocate the business of the Government of India among Ministers by assigning one or more departments to the charge of a Minister.

(3) Notwithstanding anything contained in sub-rule(1) or sub-rule(2), the President may, on the advice of the Prime Minister -

(a) associate in relation to the business allotted to a Minister under either of the said sub-rules, another Minister or Deputy Minister to perform such functions as may be assigned to him; or

(b) entrust the responsibility for specified items of business affecting any one or more than one Department to a Minister who is in charge of any other Department or to a Minister without Portfolio who is not in charge of any Department.

RAJENDRA PRASAD
PRESIDENT

---

ubstituted by Amendment series no.87 dated 26.10.1970.

Annexure III

Transaction of Business Rules

3

Provided that no orders of the nature specified in clause (c) shall be issued in respect of the Ministry of Finance without the previous concurrence of the Department of Personnel and Training.

(3) The Ministry of Law shall be consulted on-

(a) proposals for legislation;

(b) the making of rules and orders of a general character in the exercise of a statutory power conferred on the Government; and

(c) the preparation of important contracts to be entered into by the Government.

(4) Unless the case is fully covered by a decision or advice previously given by the Department of Personnel and Training that Department shall be consulted on all matters involving-

(a) the determination of the methods of recruitment and conditions of service of general application to Government servants in civil employment; and

(b) the interpretation of the existing orders of general application relating to such recruitment or conditions of service.

(5) Unless the case is fully covered by the instructions issued or advice given by that Ministry, the Ministry of External Affairs shall be consulted on all matters affecting India's external relations.

5. Requests for Papers.- (1) The Prime Minister may call for papers from any Department.

(2) The Finance Minister may call for papers from any Department in which financial consideration is involved.

(3) Any Minister may ask to see papers in any other Department if they are related to or required for the consideration of any case before him.

6. Committees of the Cabinet.-

(1) There shall be Standing Committees of the Cabinet as set out in the First Schedule to these Rules with the functions specified therein. The Prime Minister may from time to time amend the Schedule by adding to or reducing the numbers of such Committees or by modifying the functions assigned to them.

(2) Each Standing Committee shall consist of such Ministers as the Prime Minister may from time to time specify.

(3) Subject to the provisions of rule 7, each Standing Committee shall have the power to consider and take decisions on matters referred to it by order of the Minister concerned or by the Cabinet.

(4) Ad hoc Committees of Ministers including Group of Ministers may

5

THE FIRST SCHEDULE
[Rule 6(1)]

STANDING COMMITTEES OF THE CABINET AND THEIR FUNCTIONS:-

Name of the Standing Committee	Functions
1. Appointments Committee of the Cabinet.	(i) To take decisions in respect of appointments specified in Annexure I to the First Schedule to the Government of India (Transaction of Business) Rules, 1961; and to decide upon temporary upgradation of post(s) to the level of Joint Secretary and above (namely, post(s) carrying Grade Pay of Rs.10,000 in Pay Band-4 and above) for a maximum period of two years from the date of upgradation and to decide upon temporary downgradation of such post(s) for a specified period; Note: The cases of temporary upgradation or downgradation of posts are to be placed before the Appointments Committee of the Cabinet after completing requisite inter-Ministerial consultations including with the Department of Expenditure. (ii) to take decisions in respect of empanelments specified in Annexure II to the First Schedule to the Government of India (Transaction of Business) Rules, 1961; (iii) to decide all cases of disagreement relating to appointments between the Department or Ministry concerned and the Union Public Service Commission; (iv) to decide cases of extension of tenure, under the Central Staffing Scheme(s) or relevant central tenure norms, of officers belonging to the All India Services and other Group 'A' Services beyond the prescribed limits; (v) to decide cases relating to lateral shift of officers serving on Central deputation; (vi) to decide cases of premature repatriation of officers serving with the Central Government to their parent cadre or Department; (vii) to decide cases relating to inter-cadre deputation or transfer of All India Services Officers; (viii) to decide cases of extension of service beyond the age of superannuation under Fundamental Rule 56(d); (ix) to decide all cases of disagreement with the recommendations of the Search-cum-Selection Committee constituted in accordance with the statutory requirements or the relevant instructions of the

7

3. Cabinet Committee on Economic Affairs.	(i) to review on a continuous basis economic trends, problems and prospects for evolving a consistent and integrated economic policy framework for the country; (ii) to direct and co-ordinate all activities in the economic field requiring policy decisions at the highest level including foreign investment; (iii) to deal with matters relating to fixation of prices of agricultural products and price control in respect of industrial raw materials and products; (iv) to deal with increase in the prices of essential commodities or bulk goods under any form of formal or informal control; (v) to lay down priorities for public sector investment and to consider: (a) proposals for investment of more than one thousand crore rupees including those recommended by the Public Investment Board/Expenditure Finance Committee/Expanded Board of the Railways or any other appraisal fora/ committee except in cases where separate thresholds have been laid down by the Cabinet, Committee of the Cabinet or other competent authority; and (b) proposals recommended by other appraisal fora/Committee such as Public Private Partnership Appraisal Committee beyond the threshold laid down/ approved by the Competent Authority for approval by such fora but does not include proposals involving setting up of new Companies, Autonomous Bodies, Institutions, Special Purpose Vehicles, etc. or creation of posts carrying pay scale or pay band plus Grade Pay equivalent to that of a Joint Secretary to the Government of India and higher, which shall continue to be placed before the Cabinet; (vi) to consider cases of increase in the firmed up cost estimates or revised cost estimates due to reasons such as time overrun, changes in scope, under-estimation, etc. in respect of proposals that are required to be placed before the Cabinet Committee on Economic Affairs for which the procedure stipulated in the Second Schedule to the Government of India (Transaction of Business) Rules, 1961, in respect of similar cases will apply; (vii) to deal with industrial licensing policies and proposals including those relating to establishment of Joint Sector Undertakings; (viii) to review the performance of Central Public Sector

9

4. Cabinet Committee on Parliamentary Affairs.	(i) To watch the progress of Government business in Parliament and to give such directions as may be necessary from time to time, in order to secure smooth and efficient conduct of such business; (ii) to scrutinise, and to consider the attitude of the Government on non-official Bills and resolutions to be presented to Parliament; Note: The Minister of Parliamentary Affairs, may take a decision in cases, where the recommendation of the concerned Ministry/Department is that the non-official Bill/Resolution may be opposed, or the Members may be persuaded/requested to withdraw the Bill/Resolution, failing which it may be opposed. Decisions so taken by the Minister may be placed before the Cabinet Committee on Parliamentary Affairs or if no meeting of the Committee is envisaged, within a reasonable period of time, these may be circulated to the Members of the Committee for ratification. (iii) to review legislations undertaken by State Legislatures from an all-India point of view; and (iv) to consider proposals to summon or prorogue the Houses of Parliament. Note: The Committee shall, unless otherwise decided by the Cabinet Secretary, be serviced by the Ministry of Parliamentary Affairs.
5. Cabinet Committee on Political Affairs.	(i) To deal with problems relating to Centre-State relations; (ii) to consider economic and political issues that have to be judged with a wider perspective; and (iii) to deal with policy matters concerning foreign affairs that do not have external or internal security implications.

11

7. Cabinet Committee on Investment	(i) to identify key projects required to be implemented on a time-bound basis, involving investments of Rs. 1000 crore or more, or any other critical projects, as may be specified by the Committee, in sectors such as infrastructure, manufacturing, etc.; (ii) to prescribe time limits for issue of requisite approvals and clearances by the Ministries/Departments concerned in respect of projects in identified sectors; (iii) to monitor the progress of identified projects including the time prescribed/taken to obtain each approval/clearance and delays, if any; (iv) to review implementation of projects, that have been delayed beyond the stipulated timeframe, including issues causing delay in grant of clearances/approvals; (v) to review the procedures followed by Ministries/Departments to grant/refuse approvals and clearances; (vi) to take decision regarding grant/refusal of approval/ clearance of specific projects that are unduly delayed, if deemed necessary; (vii) to consider and decide measures required for expeditiously granting/refusing approvals/clearances in identified sectors including simplification of rules/procedures followed by the respective Ministries/Departments for decision making; and (viii) to require statutory authorities to discharge functions and exercise powers under the relevant law/regulation within the prescribed time frames for promoting investment and economic growth.
8. Cabinet Committee on Skill Development	(i) to provide direction and consider all policies, programmes, schemes and initiatives for skill development aimed at increasing the employability of the workforce for effectively meeting the emerging requirements of the rapidly growing economy and mapping the benefits of demographic dividend; (ii) to direct and coordinate all activities relating to skill development, enhancing workforce participation, fostering employment growth and identification and removal of the gaps between the requirements and availability of skills in different sectors; (iii) to lay down targets for expeditious implementation of all skill development initiatives by the Ministries/Departments and to periodically review the progress in this regard; and (iv) to consider any other matter relating to skill development. Note: Monetary threshold laid down for submission of cases before the Cabinet Committee on Economic Affairs shall also be followed for clearance of cases, where required, by the Cabinet Committee on Skill Development.

13

	7. Appointment to the posts of part-time non-official Directors on the Boards of Management of any State-owned public corporation, company or enterprise. 8. Appointment of Chief Vigilance Officers (CVOs) in Public Sector Undertakings, Autonomous organizations and statutory bodies, under the Central Government in the salary or salary scale or pay band plus Grade Pay equivalent to or higher than the minimum of such scale or pay band plus Grade Pay payable to a Joint Secretary to the Government of India.
B. Appointments specific to some Ministries in addition to those specified under "A" above-	
Ministry of Defence	1. Scientific Adviser to the Defence Minister. 2. Director General, Armed Forces Medical Services. 3. Director General, Ordnance Factories. 4. Additional Director General, Ordnance Factories. 5. Director General, Defence Estates. 6. Director General, Quality Assurance. 7. Additional Director General, Quality Assurance. 8. Director Grade I in Director General Quality Assurance Organisation. 9. Controller General of Defence Accounts. 10. Additional Controller General of Defence Accounts. 11. Principal Controllers of Defence Accounts and equivalent posts in Indian Defence Accounts Service. 12. Director, Institute for Defence Studies and Analyses (IDSA). ARMY 13. Chief of the Army Staff. 14. Vice-Chief of the Army Staff/General Officers Commanding-in-Chief, Central Command, Southern Command, Eastern Command, Western Command, Northern Command, South Western Command and Army Training Command.

15

ANNEXURE II TO THE FIRST SCHEDULE

EMPANELMENTS REQUIRING THE APPROVAL OF THE APPOINTMENTS COMMITTEE OF THE CABINET

1. Empanelment of officers of All India Services, and Organised Group 'A' Central Services for holding Secretariat posts at the level of Joint Secretary, Additional Secretary and Secretary in the Central Government.
2. Empanelment of officers belonging to the Central Secretariat Service for appointment to posts at the level of Joint Secretary, Additional Secretary and Secretary in the Central Government.
3. Empanelment for making appointment to posts in Grades I to III of the Indian Foreign Service.
4. Empanelment of Indian Police Service officers for holding posts at the level of Inspector General, Additional Director General and Director General or equivalent ranks in the Central Police Organisations.
5. Empanelment of Indian Forest Service Officers for holding the post of Inspector General of Forests, Additional Director General of Forests and Director General of Forests.
6. Empanelment for making appointments to the Senior Administrative Grade of organized Group 'A' Central Services other than Organised Group 'A' Services under the Ministry of Railways and Indian Telecommunications Services and other services under the Department of Telecommunications.
7. Empanelment of officers of all Central Services under the Ministry of Railways for making appointment to the posts of Additional General Manager and above in the Indian Railways.
8. Empanelment of officers of the Indian Telecommunications Services for making appointment to a post carrying a Pay Scale of Rs. 67000-(annual increment @ 3%) - 79000 and above under the Telecom Commission.
9. Empanelment for making appointments to the posts of Lieutenant General in the Indian Army and equivalent ranks in the Indian Navy, and the Indian Air Force; Director General of Armament Supply, Naval Armament Supply Officer (SAG) and Senior Director (Naval Stores) in Naval Head Quarter; and Additional Director General, Chief Engineer, Chief Architect and Chief Engineer (Quantity Surveying and Contract) in Military Engineer Services.

17

(iii) winding up, amalgamation or such other major schemes of structural re-organisation of public sector undertakings;

except in pursuance of a decision already taken by the Cabinet or the Standing Committee(s) of the Cabinet;

(iv) (1)(i) increase in the firmed up cost estimates of schemes and projects, procurement and acquisition cases relating to different departments including by the Ministry of Railways, the State owned public corporations, companies, enterprises and projects, where such increase is more than twenty percent of the original cost estimates based on feasibility report already approved by the competent authority;

(ii) cost increase due to reasons such as time overrun, changes in scope, under-estimation, etc. for the purpose of entry (iv) (1) (i) to be arrived at after excluding the escalation due to increase in statutory levies, exchange rate variation and price escalation within the original approved project time cycle;

(2) any further increase of more than five per cent in the revised cost estimates referred to in entry (iv) (1) (after excluding the escalation due to increase in statutory levies, exchange rate variation and price escalation within the approved project time cycle):

Provided that no case of revised cost estimates mentioned in entry (h) (iv) where the revised cost estimate is one thousand crore rupees or less or is within the powers delegated under second proviso to rule 7 irrespective of the authority which had initially approved the project, shall be brought before the Cabinet;

(v) Cases relating to establishment or expansion of any scheme (including any lines of production) and procurement or acquisition by any Department, State-owned public corporation, company or enterprise where such cases involve an outlay of more than one thousand crores rupees.

(i) Proposals relating to creation of all posts carrying Grade Pay of Rs.10,000 in Pay Band-4 and above.

Note.- This clause does not apply to posts in Public Sector Undertakings and scientific posts under the Flexible Complementing Scheme.

(j) Cases involving financial implications on which the Minister of Finance desires a decision of the Cabinet.

(k) Cases in which the Minister-in-Charge of the concerned department desires a decision or direction of the Cabinet in a matter of importance on a subject assigned to his charge.

(l) Cases in which a difference of opinion arises between two or more Ministers and a Cabinet decision is desired.

(m) Proposals to vary or reverse a decision previously taken by the Cabinet.

(n) Any other cases which the President or the Prime Minister may by general or special order require to be brought before the Cabinet.

THE THIRD SCHEDULE

(Rule 8)

CASES FOR SUBMISSION TO THE PRIME MINISTER AND THE PRESIDENT

Sl. No.	Nature of Cases	Reference to provision of the Constitution, if any	Authority to whom to be submitted
(1)	(2)	(3)	(4)
1.	President's emoluments, allowances, privileges and official residences.	Article 59(3)	The Prime Minister and the President.
2.	Grant of pardons, reprieves, respites, suspension, remission or commutation of a Sentence of death.	Article 72	The President.
3.	Appointment and resignation of the Prime Minister and other Ministers of the Union.	Article 75	The President.
4.	Appointment, resignation and removal of the Attorney General for India.	Article 76	The Prime Minister and the President.
5.	Nomination of members of either House of Parliament.	Articles 80 and 331	The Prime Minister and the President.
6.	Summoning or prorogation of the Houses of Parliament or dissolution of the House of the People.	Articles 85 and 108	The Prime Minister and the President.
7.	The President's address and messages to Houses of Parliament.	Articles 86 and 108	The Prime Minister and the President.
8.	Disqualifications of Members of Parliament.	Article 103	The Prime Minister and the President.
9.	Bills passed by the Houses of Parliament for the President's assent.	Article 111.	The President.
10.	Recommendations of the President for presentation to	Articles 112, 114, 115, 117 and 274.	The President.

21

Sl. No.	Nature of Cases	Reference to provision of the Constitution, if any	Authority to whom to be submitted
25.	Appointment, resignation and removal of the Chairman and Members of the Commission to investigate into conditions of backward classes.	Article 340	The Prime Minister and the President.
26.	Appointment, resignation and removal of the Chairman and Members of the Commission on Official Language of the Union.	Article 344	The Prime Minister and the President.
27.	Proclamation of Emergency and Proclamation as to financial emergency and other provisions arising out of such proclamations.	Articles 352 to 360	The Prime Minister and the President.
27A.	Declaration of commencement or cessation of a State of war.	..	The Prime Minister and the President.
28.	Recognition of Rulers of former Indian States.	Article 366(22)	The Prime Minister and the President.
29.	Amendment of the Constitution.	Article 368	The Prime Minister and the President.
30.	Proposals under Articles 370 and 371.	..	The Prime Minister and the President.
31.	Assent to Regulations made under paragraph 5(2) of the Fifth Schedule to the Constitution.	..	The President.
32.	Appointment and removal of Ambassadors, Ministers, *Charge d' Affaires* and other high dignitaries accredited to the foreign countries.	..	The Prime Minister and the President.
32A.	Grant of refusal of agreement for persons proposed to be accredited as heads of foreign diplomatic missions /High Commissions and declaring them *persona non grata*.	..	The Prime Minister and the President.
33.	Award of Medals, Decorations and "Mention in Despatches".	..	The Prime Minister and the President.

21

Sl. No.	Nature of Cases	Reference to provision of the Constitution, if any	Authority to whom to be submitted
25.	Appointment, resignation and removal of the Chairman and Members of the Commission to investigate into conditions of backward classes.	Article 340	The Prime Minister and the President.
26.	Appointment, resignation and removal of the Chairman and Members of the Commission on Official Language of the Union.	Article 344	The Prime Minister and the President.
27.	Proclamation of Emergency and Proclamation as to financial emergency and other provisions arising out of such proclamations.	Articles 352 to 360	The Prime Minister and the President.
27A.	Declaration of commencement or cessation of a State of war.	..	The Prime Minister and the President.
28.	Recognition of Rulers of former Indian States.	Article 366(22)	The Prime Minister and the President.
29.	Amendment of the Constitution.	Article 368	The Prime Minister and the President.
30.	Proposals under Articles 370 and 371.	..	The Prime Minister and the President.
31.	Assent to Regulations made under paragraph 5(2) of the Fifth Schedule to the Constitution.	..	The President.
32.	Appointment and removal of Ambassadors, Ministers, *Charge d' Affaires* and other high dignitaries accredited to the foreign countries.	..	The Prime Minister and the President.
32A.	Grant of refusal of agreement for persons proposed to be accredited as heads of foreign diplomatic missions /High Commissions and declaring them *persona non grata*.	..	The Prime Minister and the President.
33.	Award of Medals, Decorations and "Mention in Despatches".	..	The Prime Minister and the President.

THE FOURTH SCHEDULE
(Rule 10)

PERIODICAL REPORTS AND OTHER PAPERS WHICH SHALL BE SUBMITTED TO THE PRESIDENT FOR HIS INFORMATION

(1) Agenda and connected papers for meetings of the Cabinet and its Committees and cases circulated to the Ministers for recording their opinion.

(2) Record of decisions reached on cases either circulated to Ministers, or decided at a meeting of the Cabinet or any of its Committees.

(3) Monthly summaries and such other periodical returns as are required to be submitted by departments to the Cabinet.

(4) Weekly Intelligence summaries from the Director, Intelligence Bureau.

(5) Fortnightly reports about the internal political situation, etc., from States and Union Territories.

(6) Annual reports or reports submitted by officers, committees and commissions appointed either by Government or by the President in accordance with the provisions of the Constitution.

(7) Important telegrams exchanged between the Ministry of External Affairs and Representatives abroad.

(8) Copies of orders issued by departments conveying -

(a) Instructions from the President under the proviso to clause (I) of article 213 for the promulgation of ordinances by Governors of States; and

(b) Sanctions of the President under the proviso to article 304 to the introduction in the Legislature of a State of Bills or amendments imposing restrictions on the freedom of trade, commerce or intercourse with or within that State.

(9) Such other information relating to the administration of the affairs of the Union and proposals for legislation as the President may call for.

38	74/1/4/92-Cab.	03.10.1992
39	74/1/5/90-Cab.	16.10.1992
40	74/1/8/93-Cab.	31.12.1993
41	74/1/8/93-Cab.	08.03.1994
42	1/20/2/97-Cab.	26.06.1997
43	1/22/2/98-Cab.	02.07.1998
44	1/22/2/98-Cab.	27.08.1998
45	1/22/2/98-Cab.	01.12.1998
46	1/22/2/99-Cab.	18.02.2000
47	1/22/2/2001-Cab.	24.08.2001
48	1/22/2/2002-Cab.	11.02.2002
49	1/22/2/2002-Cab.	05.12.2002
50	1/22/2/2003-Cab.	26.03.2003
51	1/22/2/2004-Cab.	09.10.2004
52	1/22/2/2004-Cab.	03.05.2005
53	1/22/2/2005-Cab.	02.08.2005
54	1/22/2/2006-Cab.	01.05.2006
55	1/20/1/2007-Cab.	15.10.2007
56	1/20/1/2007-Cab.	15.10.2007
57	1/22/2/2009-Cab.	06.07.2009
58	1/20/2/2007-Cab.	16.10.2009
59	1/20/2/2009-Cab.	03.11.2009
60	1/20/2/2007-Cab.	18.01.2010
61	1/22/2/2010-Cab.	01.04.2010
62	1/22/2/2010-Cab.	08.12.2011
63	1/22/2/2012-Cab. 1/22/2/2012-Cab. corrigendum	02.01.2013 08.01.2013
64	1/22/1/2013-Cab.	10.06.2013
65	1/20/2/2014-Cab.	25.06.2014
66	1/20/6/2013-Cab.	29.08.2014
67	1/20/7/2014-Cab.	01.12.2014
68	1/20/5/2015-Cab.	11.05.2015
69	1/20/1/2016-Cab.	06.05.2016

Endnotes

Preface

1. *Calcutta Gazette/ Gazette of India*, Imperial Records, Superintendent Government Printing, India, Calcutta, 1908.
2. For more details, see Singh, Jarnail, *With Four Prime Ministers*, Konark Publishers, Delhi, 2020; Habibullah, Wajahat, *My Years with Rajiv*, Westland Books, Delhi, 2020; Singh, N.K., *Portrait of Power*, Rupa Publications, Delhi, 2020; Mukherjee, Pranab, *The Presidential Years: 2012–2017*, Rupa Publications, Delhi, 2021; and Singh, N.K., and P.K. Mishra, *Recalibrate*, Rupa Publications, Delhi, 2022.
3. Mukherjee, Pranab, *The Presidential Years: 2012–2017*, Rupa Publications, Delhi, 2021, p. 155.

Introduction

1. For details, see Jain, Ranbir Singh, *The Growth and Development of Governor Generals Executive Council*, S. Chand and Company, Delhi, 1962, pp. 13, 77, 90, 98, 118.
2. Limaye, Madhu, *Cabinet Government in India*, Radiant Publishing, Delhi, 1989, pp. 74–75.
3. Mansergh, Nicholas, and Penderel Moon (eds.), *The Transfer of Power, 1942–47*, Vol. 12, Her Majesty's Stationary Office, London, 1983, p. 766.
4. Ibid., pp. 380–381.
5. Ibid., Vol. 8, pp. 771–773.

6. Mukherjee, Rudrangshu, *Jawaharlal Nehru*, Oxford University Press, Delhi, 2019, p. 29.
7. Limaye, Madhu, op. cit., pp. 81–82.
8. Ibid., 84.
9. Vira, Dharma, *Memoirs of a Civil Servant*, Vikas Publishing House, Delhi, 1975, pp. 52–53.
10. Ambedkar, B.R., *Collected Works*, Vol. 14, Part 2, Education Department, Government of Maharashtra, Delhi, 2013, p. 1322.
11. Cited in Panandiker, V.A. Pai, and Mehra, Ajay K., *The Indian Cabinet*, Konark Publishers, Delhi, 1996, p. 34.
12. Ibid., 35.
13. Ibid.
14. Brookshire, Jerry H., 'Clement Attlee and Cabinet Reform, 1930–1945', *The Historical Journal*, Vol. 24, No. 1, 1981, p. 176.
15. Ibid.
16. Ibid., pp. 187–188.
17. Ibid., Attlee's 1932 memorandum, his draft letter to Churchill.
18. For example, see Deshmukh, B.G., 'Prime Minister's Office: We Cannot and Need Not Do Without it', *Indian Journal of Public Administration*, No. 3, 1997; Tandon, B.N., *PMO Diary-I*, Konark Publishers, Delhi, 2003, pp. xix–xx.
19. Mathai, M.O., *Reminiscences of the Nehru Age*, Vikas Publishing House, Delhi, 1978, p. 76.
20. Ibid.
21. Srivastava, C.P., *Lal Bahadur Shastri: A Life of Truth in Politics*, Oxford University Press, 1995, Delhi, p. 105.
22. Ibid., pp. 105–106.
23. Tandon, B.N., op. cit., p. xx.
24. Limaye, Madhu, op. cit., pp. 141–146.
25. See Annexure I.

26. Singh, Jarnail, *With Four Prime Ministers: My PMO Journey*, Konark Publishers, Delhi, 2020, pp. 12–13.
27. Gandhi, Gopal Krishna, 'Man who was Bharat Sarkar', *The Hindu*, 1 October 2012.
28. Sinha, Shakti, *Vajpayee: The Years that Changed India*, Penguin Random House, Delhi, 2020, p. 17.
29. Ibid.
30. According to L.K. Jha. See Singh, Karuna, 'Prime Minister's Office: A Critical Analysis', *The Indian Journal of Political Science*, Vol. 68, No. 3, 2007, p. 638.
31. Srivastava, C.P., op. cit., p. 106.
32. Deshmukh, B.G., op. cit., p. 408.

Congress Years

1. Nicholson, Mansergh, *Transfer of Power, 1942–47*, Vol. 12, H.M.S.O., London, p. 766.
2. Ibid.
3. Patel, H.M., *Rites of Passage: A Civil Servant Remembers*, Rupa Publications, Delhi, 2005, pp. 60–63, 130.
4. Patel, H.M., *The First Flush of Freedom: Recollections and Reflections*, Rupa Publications, 2005, pp. 45–52.
5. Ibid., 47.
6. Ibid., 42.
7. Ibid., 44.
8. Ibid., 48.
9. Ibid., 47.
10. Ibid., pp. 57–59.
11. Limaye, Madhu, *Cabinet Government of India*, Radiant Publishers, 1989, p. 84.

12. Ibid., 92.
13. Ibid., 57–59.
14. Shrivastava, C.P., op. cit., p. 65.
15. Ibid., 117.
16. Ibid., 67.
17. Ibid., pp. 105–106.
18. Limaye, Madhu, op. cit., pp. 56–57.
19. Gandhi, Indira, *My Truth*, Vision Books, 1981, p. 103.
20. Limaye, Madhu, op. cit., p. 117.
21. Vira, Dharma, *Memoirs of a Civil Servant*, Vikas Publishing House, Delhi, 1975, p. 89.
22. Singh, N.K., *Portraits of Power: Half a Century of being at Ringside*, Rupa Rupblications, Delhi, 2020, p. 50.
23. Mankekar, D.R., *Lal Bahadur*, p. vi; also see Gandhi, Indira, op. cit., p. 103.
24. Limaye, Madhu, op. cit., p. 117.
25. Wilson, Harold, *The Governance of Britain*, pp. 10–11.
26. Nayar, Kuldip, *Between the Lines: An Autobiography*, Roli Books, 2012, p. 21.
27. Mackintosh, John P., *The British Cabinet*, Edition 3, London, p. 519.
28. Ramesh, Jairam, *Intertwined Lives: P.N Haksar & Indira Gandhi*, Simon & Schuster, Delhi, 2019, p. 280.
29. Ibid., 272.
30. Ibid., pp. 183, 273.
31. Wilson, Harold, *The Governance of Britain*, pp. 8–9.
32. Blake, Robert, *The Prime Ministers*, Vol. 2, pp. 19–22.
33. Mackintosh, John P., op. cit., p. 519.
34. See Annexure 1.
35. Tandon, B.N., op. cit., p. xxiv.
36. Ibid., xxxii.

37. Ibid., xxiv.
38. Sengupta, Nitish K., *Inside the Steel Frame: Reminiscences and Reflections of a Former Civil Servant*, Vikas Publishing House, Delhi, 1995, p. 239.
39. Limaye, Madhu, op. cit., pp. 161–172.
40. Ibid., 169.
41. Pradhan, R.D., *My Years with Rajiv and Sonia*, Hay House, Delhi, 2014, p. 29.
42. Ibid., 260.
43. Habibullah, Wajahat, *My Years with Rajiv*, Westland Publications, Chennai, 2020, p. 19.
44. Ibid., 55.
45. Ibid.
46. Ibid., pp. 108–111.
47. Deshmukh, B.G., op. cit., p. 414.
48. Sitapati, Vinay, *Half Lion: How P.V Narasimha Rao Transformed India*, Penguin Books India, Gurugram, 2016, p. 126.
49. Ibid.
50. Baru, Sanjaya, *The Accidental Prime Minister: The Making and Unmaking of Manmohan Singh*, Penguin Books India, Delhi, 2014, p. 270.
51. Ibid., 93.
52. Ibid., pp. 94–95.
53. Ibid., pp. 100–103.
54. Ibid., 99.
55. Ibid., pp. 92–93.
56. Ibid., 99.

The Non-Congress Years

1. Limaye, Madhu, op. cit., pp. 336–337.
2. Uppal, Nishant, *Narcissus or Machiavelli? Learning Leadership from Indian Prime Ministers*, Routledge, London, 2022, p. 127.
3. Ibid., 128.
4. Sitapati, Vinay, *Jugalbandi: The BJP before Modi*, Penguin Random House, Delhi, 2020, p. 209.
5. Ibid.
6. Advani, L.K., *My Country, My Life*, Rupa Publications, Delhi, 2010, p. 575.
7. Gandhi, Gopal Krishna, 'Man who was Bharat Sarkar', *The Hindu*, 1 October 2012.
8. Sinha, Shakti, op. cit., p. 264.
9. See Annexure I.
10. Ibid.
11. Mahurkar, Uday, *Marching with a Billion: Analysing Narendra Modi's Government at Midterm*, Penguin Random House, Delhi, 2017, p. xli.
12. Ibid., 51.
13. Ibid., 59.
14. Ibid., pp. 99–103.
15. Himanta Biswa Sarma, *Facebook*, 28 April 2023, https://tinyurl.com/2s4uw5sp. Accessed on 12 March 2025.
16. Singh, N.K., and P.K. Mishra, *Recalibrate: Changing Paradigms*, Rupa Publications, Delhi, 2020, pp. 5–15.
17. Ibid.

Comparison: England, Canada, and Australia

1. Mackintosh, John P., op. cit., Vol. 2, p. 49.
2. Rose, Richard, *The Prime Minister in a Shrinking World*, Polity Press, Cambridge, 2001, p. 165.
3. Ibid., 172.
4. Ibid., 167.
5. Ibid., 171.
6. Ibid., 172.
7. Ibid., 173.
8. Hennessy, Peter, *The Prime Minister*, Allen Lane, London, 2000, p. 7.
9. Ibid., 9.
10. Ibid., 147.
11. Ibid., 155.
12. Ibid., 56.
13. Ibid., 476.
14. Ibid., 487.
15. Kavanagh, Dennis, and Anthony Seldon, *The Powers Behind the Prime Minister*, HarperCollins Publishers, London, 1999, pp. 44–45, 79.
16. Lewis, J.P., 'Elite Attitude on the Centralization of Power in Canadian Political Executive', *Canada Journal of Political Science*, 2013, pp. 802–803.
17. Ibid., 816.
18. Clark, Joe, 'The Canadian Prime Ministership', *Presidential Studies Quarterly*, Vol. 2, No. 1, 1981, p. 32.
19. Ibid., 33.
20. Ibid., 41.
21. Courtney, John C., 'Has the Canadian Prime Minister became

"Presidentialized"?', *Presidential Studies Quarterly*, Vol. 14, No. 2, 1984, pp. 240–241.

22. Ibid., p. 239.
23. Simeon, James C., op. cit., p. 561.
24. Ibid., 573.
25. O'Malley, Eoin, 'The Power of Prime Ministers: Results of an Experts Survey', *International Political Science Review*, Vol. 28, No. 1, 2007, pp. 17–18.
26. Wanna, John (ed.), *Critical Reflections on Australian Public Policy*, ANU Press, Canberra, 2009, p. 81.
27. O'Malley, Eoin, op. cit., p. 17.
28. Wanna, John, op. cit., p. 78.
29. Ibid., 74.
30. Rhodes, R.A.W. (ed.), *The Australian Study of Politics*, Palgrave Macmillan, London, 2009, p. 125.
31. Rhodes, R.A.W., and Patrick Duan Leavy, *Prime Minister, Cabinet and Core Executive*, Palgrave Macmillan, Hamshire, 1995, p. 13.
32. Ibid., 14.
33. Ibid., 56.

Conclusion

1. Limaye, Madhu, op. cit., p. 74.
2. Ibid., 75.

Bibliography

Advani, L. K., *My Country, My Life*, Rupa Publications, Delhi, 2010.

Ambedkar, B. R., *Collected Works*, Vol. 14, Part 2, Education Department, Government of Maharashtra, Delhi, 2013.

Baru, Sanjaya, *The Accidental Prime Minister: The Making and Unmaking of Manmohan Singh*, Penguin Random House, Delhi, 2014.

Blake, Robert, *The Prime Ministers*, Heinemann, London, 1966.

Brookshire, Jerry H., 'Clement Attlee and Cabinet Reform, 1930–1945', *The Historical Journal*, Vol. 24, No. 1, 1981, pp. 175–188.

Calcutta Gazette/Gazette of India, Imperial Records Calcutta, Superintendent Government Printing, India, 1908.

Clark, Joe, 'The Canadian Prime Ministership', *Presidential Studies Quarterly*, Vol. 11, No. 1, 1981, pp. 32–43.

Courtney, John C., 'Has the Canadian Prime Minister Become "Presidentialized"?', *Presidential Studies Quarterly*, Vol. 14, No. 2, 1984, pp. 238–241.

Deshmukh, B. G., 'Prime Minister's Office—We Cannot and Need Not Do Without It', *Indian Journal of Public Administration*, No. 3, 1997, pp. 13–28.

Gandhi, Gopal Krishna, 'Man Who Was Bharat Sarkar', *The Hindu*, 1 October 2012.

Gandhi, Indira, *My Truth*, Vision Books, Delhi, 1981.

Habibullah, Wajahat, *My Years with Rajiv: Triumph and Tragedy*, Westland Books, Chennai, 2020.

Hennessy, Peter, *The Prime Minister*, Allen Lane, London, 2000.

Jain, Ranbir Singh, *The Growth and Development of Governor General's Executive Council*, S. Chand and Company, Delhi, 1962.

Singh, Karuna, 'Prime Minister's Office: A Critical Analysis', *The Indian Journal of Political Science*, Vol. 68, No. 3, 2007, pp. 629–640.

Kavanagh, Dennis, and Anthony Seldon, *The Powers Behind the Prime Minister*, HarperCollins Publishers, London, 1999.

Lewis, J.P., 'Elite Attitudes on the Centralization of Power in Canadian Political Executives: A Survey of Former Canadian Provincial and Federal Cabinet Ministers, 2000–2010', *Canadian Journal of Political Science*, Vol. 46, No. 4, 2013, pp. 799–819.

Limaye, Madhu, *Cabinet Government in India*, Radiant Publishing, New Delhi, 1989.

Mackintosh, John P., *The British Cabinet*, Edition 3, Stevens & Sons, London, 1977.

Mackintosh, Robert James, *Memoirs of the Life of Sir James Mackintosh*, Vol. 2, Edward Moxon and Co., London, 1836.

Mahurkar, Uday, *Marching with a Billion: Analysing Narendra Modi's Government at Midterm*, Penguin Random House, Delhi, 2017.

Mankekar, D. R., *Builders of Modern India: Lal Bahadur Shastri*, Publications Division, Ministry of Information and Broadcasting, Delhi, 1973.

Mankekar, D.R., and Kamla Mankekar, *Decline and Fall of Indira Gandhi*, Vision Books, Delhi, 1977.

Mansergh, Nicholas, and Penderel Moon (eds.), *The Transfer of Power, 1942–47*, Vol. 12, Her Majesty's Stationery Office, London, 1983.

Mathai, M. O., *Reminiscences of the Nehru Age*, Vikas Publishing House, Delhi, 1978.

Mukherjee, Pranab, *The Presidential Years: 2012–2017*, Rupa Publications, Delhi, 2021.

Mukherjee, Rudrangshu, *Jawaharlal Nehru*, Oxford University Press, Delhi, 2019.

Nayar, Kuldip, *Between the Lines: An Autobiography*, Roli Books, Chennai, 2012.

O'Malley, Eoin, 'The Power of Prime Ministers: Results of an Experts Survey', *International Political Science Review*, Vol. 28, No. 1, 2007, pp. 17–18.

Pai Panandiker, V.A., and Ajay K. Mehra, *The Indian Cabinet*, Konark Publishers, Delhi, 1996.

Patel, H.M., *Rites of Passage: A Civil Servant Remembers*, Rupa Publications, Delhi, 2005.

Patel, H.M., *The First Flush of Freedom: Recollections and Reflections*, Rupa Publications, Delhi, 2005.

Pradhan, R. D., *My Years with Rajiv and Sonia*, Hay House, Delhi, 2014.

Ramesh, Jairam, *Intertwined Lives: P.N. Haksar and Indira Gandhi*, Simon & Schuster, Delhi, 2019.

Rhodes, R.A.W., and Patrick Duan Leavy (eds.), *Prime Minister, Cabinet and Core Executive*, Palgrave Macmillan, Hampshire, 1995.

Rhodes, R.A.W. (ed.), *The Australian Study of Politics*, Palgrave Macmillan, Hampshire, 2009.

Rose, Richard, *The Prime Minister in a Shrinking World*, Polity Press, Cambridge, 2001.

Sengupta, Nitish K., *Inside the Steel Frame: Reminiscences and Reflections of a Former Civil Servant*, Vikas Publishing House, Delhi, 1995.

Himanta Biswa Sarma, *Facebook*, 28 April 2023, https://tinyurl.com/2s4uw5sp. Accessed on 12 March 2025.

Simeon, James C., 'Prime Minister's Office and White House Office: Political Administration in Canada and the United States', *Presidential Studies Quarterly*, Vol. 21, No. 3, 1991, pp. 559–80.

Singh, Jarnail, *With Four Prime Ministers: My PMO Journey*, Konark Publishers, Delhi, 2020.

Singh, N.K., *Portraits of Power: Half a Century of Being at Ringside*, Rupa Publications, Delhi, 2020.

Singh, N.K., and P.K. Mishra, *Recalibrate: Changing Paradigms*, Rupa Publications, Delhi, 2020.

Sinha, Shakti, *Vajpayee: The Years That Changed India*, Penguin Random House, Delhi, 2020.

Sitapati, Vinay, *Half Lion: How P.V. Narasimha Rao Transformed India*, Penguin Books India, Gurugram, 2016.

Sitapati, Vinay, *Jugalbandi: The BJP before Modi*, Penguin Random House, Delhi, 2020.

Srivastava, C. P., *Lal Bahadur Shastri: A Life of Truth in Politics*, Oxford University Press, Delhi, 1995.

Tandon, B.N., *PMO Diary–I: Prelude to the Emergency*, Konark Publishers, Delhi, 2003.

Uppal, Nishant, *Narcissus or Machiavelli?*, Routledge, London, 2022.

Vira, Dharma, *Memoirs of a Civil Servant*, Vikas Publishing House, Delhi, 1975.

Wanna, John (ed.), *Critical Reflections on Australian Public Policy*, ANU Press, Canberra, 2009.

Wilson, Harold, *The Governance of Britain*, Weidenfeld & Nicolson, London, 1976.

Index

acquisition, 49
administrative reforms, 6
Ahluwalia, Montek Singh, 21, 25
Aiyangar, 45
Aiyer, Mani Shankar, 21
Alexander, P.C., xii, xl, 20, 21, 46, 101, 102
Allocation of Business Rule, 63
Ambedkar, xxvii, 106, 110
American president, xxii, xxv, xxvii, 87, 108, 110
annual budget, 64
Arora, G.K., 21

babus, xxxviii, xxxix
Baldwin, 78, 81
Baru, Sanjay, xviii, xlii, 31, 32, 37
benevolence, xxx
biographies, xli
Blair, Tony, xi, 49, 76, 79, 105
Bose, Subhash, 8
Brecher, Michael, xxxiii
British tradition, xi, 23
Brown, Gordon, xi, 105
Brownlow Committee, 86
Butler, Rob, 77

cabinet colleagues, xxi, xxii, xxvi, xxviii, xxxiv, 39, 82, 94, 100, 101, 102
campaigns, xxvii, xxviii
Carter, Jimmy, 86
CDS, 63
Central Bureau of Investigation, xxxvii
Central Services Board, 68
chancellor, 78
Chandra, Naresh, 27, 35
Chatterjee, Pulok, 33
checkmate, 12
checks and balances, xxxii
Churchill, Winston, xxviii, 78, 80
civil government, 2
civil-military, 2
Clark, Joe, 83
Coates, Eric, 2
Code of Conduct, 7
collegial functioning, 81, 94, 95
commander-in-chief, 2
commanding, xxxix, 8, 52, 110
command premiership, 79, 80
Committee of Secretaries, 25
committee system, 78, 92, 94, 106

Common Minimum Programme, xiii, 33, 37, 50
Constituent Assembly, xv
constitutional amendment, xxiii
Conventions, 51, 96
conveyers, xxxiii
coordinating ministers, xxxi
core group, 32
corporate affairs, 53
Courtney, John, 85
Cross Road, xxiii

Damodaran, Raman, 27
Das, Durga, xli
democratization, x, xvi, xxviii, 88, 89, 91
Department of Enforcement, xxxvii
Desai, Morarji, xii, xxxiv, xxxvii, 6, 12, 21, 23, 41, 53
Deshmukh, B.G., xliii, 21, 49
Dhar, P.C., xii
Dhawan, R.K., 32
discourse, 77, 83, 96, 97
Disraeli, 81
Dixit, J.N., 28, 33
domineering, 8, 94, 96, 97
dynasties, xxx, 19, 20, 27

Economic Advisory Council, xliv
EGOMs, 32, 63
Emergency, xxx, xxxiv, 4, 18, 39, 40, 41, 42, 43
Executive Council, ix, xix, xxii
ex-officio, xxiii
external affairs, xiii, xix, 33, 34, 93
extra-constitutional, xxxviii, xlii, 64

Fernandes, George, 43
Fernandes, Oscar, 24
foreign policy, xviii, 30, 45, 51, 52, 53, 63
Fotedar, M.L., 31
FPRO, 86
Fraser, Malcom, 90

Gaekwad, Sayajirao, 66
Gandhi, Gopal Krishna, xxxix, 52
Gandhi, Indira, xi, xii, xiv, xv, xvii, xviii, xxv, xxvii, xxviii, xxix, xxxiii, xxxiv, xxxv, xxxvii, xliii, 4, 9, 10, 11, 12, 13, 14, 15, 16, 17, 18, 20, 21, 22, 23, 24, 25, 27, 28, 31, 32, 33, 34, 39, 40, 41, 42, 44, 45, 46, 50, 51, 53, 56, 58, 60, 65, 100, 102
Gandhi, Rajiv, xii, xiii, xvii, xxxviii, xlii, 10, 17, 20, 21, 22, 24, 25, 26, 27, 28, 30, 32, 33, 40, 50, 56, 64, 100, 101
Gandhi, Sonia, xii, xiii, xxviii, 22, 29, 30, 31, 32, 33, 35, 36, 56, 57
George, David Lloyd, 81
George, Vincent, 32, 56
Ghatate, N.M., 51
ghost file, xxxvi, 64
Gladstone, 81

Gopal, S., xlii
Gorton, John, 93
Gowda, Dev, xl, 47, 48
grassroots cadres, 20
Grewal, Sarla, 21, 101
Gujarat experience, 67
Gujral, I.K., 47, 48

Habibullah, Wajahat, x, xlii, 24
Haksar, P.N., xi, xl, xliv, 11, 13, 41
Heath, Edward, 81
hierarchy, xxi, xxxviii, xliii, 4, 9, 19, 32, 51, 100, 101
House of Commons, 77
Howard, John, 90
Hughes, Billy, 90

ideological, 54
interim government, ix, xix, xxi, xxii, xxiv, xxv, 1
Ismay, Lord, xxi, 1

Janata government, 43, 44
Jha, L.K., xxxiii, xxxix, xl, 8, 10, 11, 13, 16, 17, 18, 34, 39, 41, 42, 60
Jha, R.R., xliii
Joshi, Hiren, 61
judicial killings, xxiii
Jugalbandi, xli

Kamaraj Plan, xxix, 5, 12, 20, 23, 27, 44
kar sevaks, 28
Keatings, Paul, 90
Kulkarni, Sudheendra, 51
Kumar, Prabhat, 52

legitimacy, xxv, 84
leviathan, xii, 5, 8, 24
liaison, 86
Limaye, Madhu, xli, 11, 25
lineage, x
lobbyists, 66
Lok Sabha, xv, xxviii, xxxv, xxxix, 22, 28, 40, 47, 48, 102

Mahajan, Pramod, 52
Major, John, 79
marginalization, xvi, xxiv, xlii, 4, 5, 7, 12
Martin, Paul, 87
Maruti project, 17
mass spectacle, 62
Mathai, M.O., xli, 32
mechanics men, xxxiii
media advisor, xviii, xxxv
memoirs, xxxix, xli, xlii
Menon, V.P., xxi
Miliband, David, 76
military, xx, xxi, 2, 4, 64, 86
mini government, xxxiv
Ministry of Finance, xxxvii
Mishra, Brajesh, xxxix, xl, 36, 37, 49, 51, 52, 53, 56, 101
Mishra, L.N., 19
Mishra, Nripendra, 57, 58, 60, 101

Modi, Narendra, 47, 57
monarch, xxii, 22, 79
Mountbatten, xix, xxi, 1, 2

Nair, T.K.A., 33, 101
National Advisory Council, xiii, xxviii, 31
National Front, 40, 47
National Informatics Centre, 24
National Security Advisor, xiii, xxxv, 33
National Security Board, 52
Nayar, Kuldip, 11
NCMP, 33
Nehru, Arun, 26
Nehru, Motilal, xxv, 13
Nehru regime, xi
Nehruvian, 19
NGO, xxxviii
NITI Aayog, xiv, 69
NMML, xviii
nomenclature, xxxiv, xxxv, 7, 8, 21, 39, 46
nuclearization, xv

office of record, xxxvi, xxxvii

Panandiker, V.A. Pai, xli
Pandit, R.V., 51
pan-Indian, xxix, xxx
Pant, Govind Ballabh, 13
Parthasarathy, G., 21
Patel, Ahmad, 24
Patel, H.M., xxi, xxii, 1, 3, 5
Patel, Sardar, xxi, xli, 4, 42
Pawar, Sharad, 31
perception management, 60
Pitroda, Sam, 21
Plan, Kamraj, xxix, 5, 12, 20, 23, 27
Planning Commission, 14, 21, 27
Platonic idea, 77
plebiscitary, xvi, xxvii, 19
PMH, xii, xxxiv, xxxviii, xlii, xliii, 14, 17, 18, 19, 22
PMS, ix, xi, xii, xiv, xv, xvi, xvii, xix, xxi, xxii, xxiii, xxiv, xxv, xxvi, xxvii, xxviii, xxix, xxxi, xxxii, xxxiii, xxxiv, xxxvii, xxxviii, xli, xlii, xliii, xliv, 1, 2, 3, 5, 6, 7, 8, 9, 10, 11, 12, 13, 14, 15, 16, 17, 18, 19, 21, 22, 23, 33, 34, 35, 38, 39, 41, 44, 45, 46, 49, 59, 63, 64, 78, 81, 99, 100, 101, 102, 106
policy unit, 41, 81
political boss, 14
portfolio, xix, xx, xxiv, 5, 6, 16, 30, 33, 90
power centre, xii, xiii, 27, 32
PPS, xi, xvii, xxi, xxii, xxvi, xxxiii, xxxv, xliv, 1, 7, 16, 39, 45, 46, 78, 81, 90, 93, 105, 106
Pradhan, R.D., 22
Prasad, H.Y. Sharada, 18
presidential, 65, 75, 82, 84, 85, 91
prime ministerial, x, xi, xiii, xiv, xv, xvi, xxii, xxiii, xxiv, xxv,

xxvi, xxvii, xxviii, xxix, xxx, xxxi, xxxii, xxxviii, xliv, 5, 6, 10, 11, 14, 25, 27, 36, 37, 38, 46, 50, 54, 55, 60, 74, 76, 77, 78, 80, 81, 82, 83, 84, 85, 87, 88, 89, 91, 93, 95, 96, 100, 102, 103, 105, 106, 107, 108, 109, 110
primus inter pares, 38, 79, 100, 102, 107
Privy Council Office, 82, 83, 87
procedures, xiv, xxxvi, 4, 7, 17, 38, 42, 69, 88, 91

Quebec, Francophone, 84

Race Course Road, 32, 52
Raisina Hill, 34
Ramesh, Jairam, 28
Rann of Kutch, 9
Rao, G.V.K., 46
Rao, Narasimha, 48, 49
Rasgotra, M.S., xviii

Sangh, Jan, 43
Senate, 85, 86
Sen, Ronen, 21
Shankar, Vidya, xii, xli, 40, 41, 42, 46
Sharma, Satish, 27
Shastri, Lal Bahadur, xxiii, 6
Shekhar, Chandra, 47, 48
Shimla Agreement, 14
Singh, Charan, 40, 43, 46, 48, 101
Singh, Jarnail, x, xviii
Singh, Karuna, xliii
Singh, Manmohan, xii, xiv, xvii, xviii, xxviii, xlii, 21, 22, 30, 31, 32, 33, 35, 37, 38, 48, 57, 58
Singh, T.P., 9, 17
Singh, Vir Bhadra, 26
Singh, V.P., xxx, 25, 47, 48
single-window clearance, xii
Sinha, Amarjeet, 61
Sinha, Shakti, xviii, xli, xlii, 52
social movements, xxix, xxx
special prerogatives, 85
special secretary, 18
Srivastava, C.P., xlii
structuralist, xli
super cabinet, xxxiv, 41
Swadeshi Jagran Manch, 56
syndicate, 12, 44

Tandon, Bishan, 19, 51
Tandon, B.N., xxxiii, xlii
technologies, 55, 61
Thakkar, Jagdish, 61
Thakur, Janardan, xlii
Thatcher, Margaret, xi, 49, 76, 105
Thengadi, Dattopant, 56
think tanks, 63
Trudeau, Pierre, 82, 87

United Kingdom, 2

Vajpayee government, xiii, 37, 50
Varma, Amar Nath, 27
Vasudavan, R., 21

viceroy, xix, xx, xxii, 1, 2, 16, 99
Vira, S.S. Dharma, xli
Vohra, N.N., xviii

warrant of precedence, xiv, 13, 16, 35
Wavell, Lord, ix, xxii
Weller, Patrick, 91
Westminster, xxiv, 89, 94, 95
White House Office, 86
Williams, Marcia, 12
Wilson, Harold, xlii, 11
World War, xix, 55, 81

Yew, Lee Kuan, 66